10/6/1

How to Make Good Curries

Helen Lawson

Hamlyn
London · New York · Sydney · Toronto

Contents

First published in the Leisure Plan Series in 1970
by The Hamlyn Publishing Group Limited
London · New York · Sydney · Toronto
Astronaut House, Feltham, Middlesex, England
Second edition 1973
Reprinted 1974
© Copyright The Hamlyn Publishing Group Limited 1973

ISBN 0 600 34408 8
Printed by Cox and Wyman Ltd, Fakenham, England

Jacket picture by courtesy of the
American Rice Council
Photograph by John Lee shows
Vegetable meat curry (see page 48)

Illustrations by Jackie Grippaudo

ACKNOWLEDGEMENT

The following colour photograph is by
courtesy of:

WHITE FISH AUTHORITY
Curried fillets of sole, *page 27*

Introduction

Although the art of curry-making originated in India, this is not an Indian cookery book. For, just as Indian cuisine embraces many other delights as well as curries, so there are other great curry producing countries.

The word 'curry' comes from the Hindustani word: *turcarri*. In the colloquial it is shortened to *turri*; in Anglo-Saxon usage it became 'curry'. Curry still forms the one main meal of the day for the vast majority of millions of Indians and Pakistanis. But the art of curry-making has spread through Burma, Malaysia, and around the East coast up as far as Hong Kong.

Most of the great curries of the world come from South-East Asia – the countries of India, Pakistan, Ceylon, Burma, Thailand, Malaysia, and Indonesia.

The curries, whether mild, hot, liquid, or dry, are a subtle blending of spices intended to enhance, not overpower, the flavour of the main ingredients.

As a start, you can use commercial curry powders when making curry, but you could supplement it with several of the spices that go into most blends of curry powder i.e., cumin, coriander, ground or fresh green ginger, cardamom etc., adding or subtracting until you have the blend which suits you best. For the art of curry-making lies not in hot spicing but in the delicacy of flavour blending.

This book includes classic curries from all the countries mentioned, as well as ones which have been adapted in the West and Antipodes.

If you start with the Western-type recipes and develop a taste for good curries, you might become experimental and try out the dishes with more subtle spicing. In time you will notice how curries can vary very much according to the ingredients of their country of origin.

Burma. Burmese curries are not highly spiced, although garlic is used generously. The Burmese are Buddhists, and rice is the staple diet, but fish and vegetables are used in abundance.

Ceylon. The Ceylonese can be broadly divided into three groups: the indigenous race known as the Sinhalese, who are Buddhists and vegetarians; the Tamil Indians, from India, who have been fishermen for centuries, and whose curries naturally feature fish; the Burghers, Christian descendants of the Dutch and Portuguese settlers, whose curries are rich and spicy. All make good use of the abundance of coconuts on the island, and a speciality of Ceylonese curries is the use of coconut milk as stock. Tradition-

ally, Ceylonese curries are very hot; *chilli powder* is not incorporated in the spices blended to make curry powder, but is always added separately; this enables each household to adjust the hotness of the curry according to taste. Ceylon also produces some of the best *cinnamon* in the world, and this spice is included in most of their curries.

China. The Chinese, who are some of the best cooks in the world, certainly connoisseurs of good food, have their own curry style. Chinese curry is usually pan-fried in a dry frying pan, using a low flame, for Chinese chefs believe this really brings out the true flavour of curry. The trick is to stir constantly to prevent it burning.

India. In such a vast country, with varying climatic and agricultural conditions, it is natural to expect a great variation in curries also. The people are mostly vegetarians, although there are certain castes who eat poultry and eggs. In the north, curries are mild, like those of Pakistan. From the lovely valley of Kashmir come the few Indian curries that contain fruit. The inhabitants of Bengal are mostly vegetarians and rely greatly on spices to make delicious curries out of the vegetables obtainable. Aubergine is one of the most commonly used vegetables in Bengali curries. The farther south you travel in India, the hotter the curries become. In Madras, chillis grow abundantly and are used liberally. Madras curries are therefore much hotter than those of the north.

Indonesia. Compared with Indian curries, those from Indonesia contain relatively few spices. Coconuts are plentiful; coconut milk is used in nearly all curries and coconut oil is the common cooking oil. Hot chillis are used often.

Malaysia. As in Ceylon, coconuts are plentiful, and many Malayan curries are made with a stock of coconut milk. Tamarind, a sweet-sour fruit pulp, and *blachan*, a dark paste made with shrimps or prawns, give varying flavours to their curries. Chinese and Indians went to the country in great numbers in the nineteenth century to work in the tin mines and rubber plantations. The Indians brought their curries; the Chinese influence can be seen in the delicious satays for which Malaysia is famous.

Pakistan. Curries are usually mild but rich – yogurt, sour cream, and goat's milk are often used to thicken the gravies. Most Pakistanis are Moslems and consider the pig an unclean animal; therefore pork curries are not eaten in Pakistan. Rice is a traditional curry accompaniment but, as wheat is grown abundantly, different types of unleavened breads such as chapatis and puris are often served in place of rice.

Thailand. Like the Burmese, the Thais are Buddhists and rice is their staple diet. The country is threaded with many waterways and canals, thus bringing an abundance of fish. Thai curries are not heavily spiced, but many are seasoned with pungent fish or prawn sauces.

Spices and herbs for curry

The curative powers of spices, as much as taste, was probably responsible originally for their use with food. Information about the medicinal qualities of spices was more general knowledge a few hundred years ago than in this age of universal education. Ginger, for instance, is a wonderful stomachic. Henry VIII was well aware of this, and on one occasion sent it to the poor and sick of London. Turmeric is used for sterilising. Cumin was especially imported by the Ancient Egyptians from India to preserve their mummies. Spices became known to Europe of the Middle Ages as a preservative of food and meat in the days of no refrigeration.

The majority of Orientals use different spices in varying proportions for each dish; these are often bought ready-mixed in the market places. They do not have a 'curry flavour', but a changing scale based on the curry theme. Vegetables, meat, fish and eggs all have a different blend of spices to emphasize the basic flavours of the main ingredients.

Once you have tried cooking with your own blends of individual spices, you will not want to use packaged curry powder again. Also, you will find it more economical and easier in the long run. Spices are always stronger in dried form, and the seed form keeps better than the powdered, but is liable to rot in a damp place.

In all the curry recipes given, curry powder or paste may be used to replace the spices mentioned. How much you use depends on whether you like a hot or mild curry. To a pint of liquid use plus or minus one tablespoon curry powder. With dry curries, work out a measure equivalent to the separate spices given. Remember that curry powder develops strength in cooking.

To blend a good curry powder of your own, there are a few rules that must be followed.

First, all spices must be fresh. The taste which a lot of Westerners dislike comes from using stale old curry powder. In and around most large cities there are a number of authentic Indian shops where it is easy to get most ingredients for curries.

Second, all spices used in blending your own curry powder should be purchased whole. If the spice is the kind which comes in a pod or husk, like the cardamom, this should be left whole for grinding. Certain curries, too, call for inclusion of spices unground, such as cinnamon stick, a finger of ginger, whole peppercorns, cloves, etc.

Third, all curry powder must be cooked before adding to other ingredients. This is perhaps the most important rule for the beginner in curry-making, and one which is often disregarded. This rule applies whether merely adding a pinch of raw curry powder at the last minute to a soup, or mixing it with cream cheese for a canapé. In every use the curry powder should be fried well in a small amount of heated fat. These are the chief spices and herbs used:

Allspice is also known as the Jamaica Pepper. The berry is a small, hard, black seed resembling a peppercorn. It has the blended flavour of cloves, nutmeg and cinnamon and is used largely for flavourings, especially for pickles, soups, stews. It is used in many curry powder blends. Can be bought whole or ground.

Aniseed is the small, dried seed of anise, a plant similar to parsley. It has a strong liquorice flavour. A spoonful of ground aniseed is usually passed in polite circles after a heavy curry. Each person takes a pinch, puts it on the tip of his tongue to aid digestion.

Bay leaves from a species of laurel tree, are added, fresh or dried, to stews or curries, and usually removed before the dish is served. They have a pungent aromatic flavour and should be used sparingly.

Caraway seed is similar to anise in appearance. An important addition to curry powder. Usually comes as whole seeds, sometimes ground.

Cardamom is often called the Seed of Paradise because of its delicate flavour and aroma as well as its exhilarating effect on the user. A small pod slightly larger than a pea with a papery husk has many brown seeds inside. An Indian cook discards the husk as she grinds the spice, but if the pods are used in a recipe to be cooked for any length of time, the husk will dissolve.

Cinnamon is the aromatic bark of any of several kinds of lauraceous trees. This is probably the most popular of all spices used in Western cooking. It is available in stick form or ground.

Cloves are the dried unopened buds of a tropical tree of the myrtle family. Used in the Orient to disinfect sick rooms and also used today in Western deodorants. A most powerful spice – one clove too many will spoil the curry powder, but used with care, it improves many dishes. Comes whole or ground.

Coriander seeds have a sweet lemon flavour and can

be used to flavour puddings, cakes, etc. They have been popular in the East for over 7,000 years. Mexicans use them to flavour their soups. Coriander is added to curry powder as it is supposed to prevent flatulence. Seeds come whole or ground.

Cumin is an aromatic seed. It was used as a tithe or tax as far back as the days of Christ. Used all over the world in bread, cakes, pies and other baked goods. Available whole or ground.

Fennel is a herb belonging to the carrot family, though in the case of one variety the base is shaped like celery and has an onion texture. Tastes a little like aniseed. Excellent in fish sauces. Fresh seeds, dried seeds and ground fennel are used in curries.

Fenugreek known as Greek hay, is a plant of the pea family. Seeds have a sweet flavour like maple sugar. Used not only in curry powders, but in the manufacture of sweets.

Ginger comes from a fragrant tropical plant. The part used as a spice is the root. This is used fresh or dried (the first is known as 'green', although it is not that colour). Ground ginger is used as a condiment and in many medicines. It is one of the more important spices used for curry blending. Add a pinch of ginger rather than hot peppers for making a curry hotter.

Mace, an aromatic spice from the fibrous covering of nutmeg, is used ground in milk puddings, and pickles, also in curry powder. Shreds of husk are called 'blades of mace'.

Mint, a herb native to Asia, is used throughout the East. There are more than 30 species of this plant. It is added in a paste form to many Hindu curries. Can be grown fresh almost anywhere.

Mustard seeds are used whole in the making of pickles and curry powders. There are several varieties. Seeds come whole; when ground called dry mustard.

Nutmeg is the large seed of a peachlike evergreen tree. Indians use this spice in curries, and in other preparations as well. Nutmegs are available whole; when ground, it is called grated nutmeg.

Peppers are also called pimento or pepperone, and can be green, yellow and red, hot or sweet. The ones used in recipes in this book are the sweet variety and easily obtained.

Chilli peppers are called chillis in the text. They can be used fresh, but are more familiar as dried. *Chilli powder* which often replaces fresh chillis in a recipe is usually a combination of hot and milder chillis and sometimes other herbs.

Paprika is made by grinding the dried pods of the sweet, mild pepper.

Cayenne peppers are the most pungent, and very hot, made from grinding dried seeds and red pods.

Pepper is a climbing shrub. The peppercorns make the most popular spice in the world. Black pepper is unripe berries dried in the sun. White pepper is the same berries left to ripen on the bush. Both kinds come whole or ground.

Poppy seeds which are used whole or ground, have a nutlike flavour and a crunchy texture. A favourite addition to curry powder blends.

Saffron, the rarest and most exotic of spices, is the stigma of the mauve autumn crocus blossom. All over the world it is in great demand not only for dyes, but for flavourings for confections, pastries, etc. In the East it is most highly prized for curry powder, but as it takes about 75,000 stigmas to make a pound of saffron, it is used only on special occasions. Turmeric is used often as a substitute. Saffron comes in cake form, as dried stigmas, or ground and bottled. One pinch goes a long way.

Sesame seeds come from tall, beanlike pods and have a pleasing nut flavour, and can sometimes be used instead of almonds. They are often blended in curry powders. They are also pressed to make oil.

Turmeric belongs to the ginger family. As with ginger, the part used is the root, but turmeric has a more brilliant colour and a much sweeter and more delicate flavour than ginger. It is often used as a substitute for saffron. Usually available ground.

Curry powder – blends

The proper blending of curry powder, like that of the rest of the ingredients for the dish, requires time, experiment and patience, but it gives the creative cook the satisfaction of finding exactly what is best for her and therefore truly individual. Grind the spices together in a mortar, but sprinkle with vinegar and water while mixing to keep down the fine dust; this is done to protect the eyes. If using an electric grinder, it, too, should be kept covered when in use.

Taste individual spices in food and you will get to know them better. Knowing the spices will make your curry cooking more fun and more varied. No two dishes will taste the same, because no two are spiced in the same way.

Buy ready-made curry powder from a specialist shop, rather than a packed variety from a local grocer or supermarket. You will find that a shop dealing with Oriental foods and spices will have more than one blend of curry powder, and will advise you on what you need. If you are buying one blend for all-round use, better to have a mild one and add ginger and/or chilli powder to make it hotter. A blend that is red in colour is usually hot, having a goodly proportion of chilli in it, and it could have too much for your taste. If you like a red-looking curry which is not too hot, add some paprika when you are cooking the spices.

When curry powder is given in recipes in this book, a good basic blend is called for, either one recommended at your specialist shop or one you have mixed yourself. If you use a packed variety, unless it is labelled 'Madras' or 'hot', you will probably find you need about twice as much as given in the recipe, especially if it is very light in colour. Below are some curry powder blends you can make yourself; try them out in curries, and as you become more experienced you might add to or subtract from the ingredients, according to the tastes you develop.

Curry powder 1

A fairly mild basic blend

IMPERIAL	METRIC	AMERICAN
4 oz. ground turmeric	110 g. ground turmeric	1 cup ground turmeric
4 oz. coriander seeds	110 g. coriander seeds	1⅓ cups coriander seeds
4 oz. cumin seeds	110 g. cumin seeds	1 cup cumin seeds
3 oz. dried root ginger	80 g. dried root ginger	3 oz. dried root ginger
2 peppercorns	2 peppercorns	2 peppercorns
1 cardamom pod	1 cardamom pod	1 cardamom pod
1 dried red chilli	1 dried red chilli	1 dried red chili
1 oz. saffron (optional)	25 g. saffron (optional)	1 oz. saffron (optional)
½ oz. mustard seeds	15 g. mustard seeds	1½ tablespoons mustard seeds

Curry powder 2

A more robust basic blend

IMPERIAL	METRIC	AMERICAN
4 oz. ground turmeric	110 g. ground turmeric	1 cup ground turmeric
4 oz. coriander seeds	110 g. coriander seeds	1⅓ cups coriander seeds
4 oz. cumin seeds	110 g. cumin seeds	1 cup cumin seeds
2 oz. dried root ginger	50 g. dried root ginger	2 oz. dried root ginger
2 peppercorns	2 peppercorns	2 peppercorns
1 oz. cardamom pods	25 g. cardamom pods	1 oz. cardamom pods
1 oz. fennel seeds	25 g. fennel seeds	¼ cup fennel seeds
1 oz. dried red chillis	25 g. dried red chillis	¼ cup dried red chilis
1 oz. blades of mace	25 g. blades of mace	¼ cup blades of mace
½ oz. whole cloves	15 g. whole cloves	1½ tablespoons whole cloves
½ oz. mustard seeds	15 g. mustard seeds	2 tablespoons mustard seeds
½ oz. poppy seeds	15 g. poppy seeds	2 tablespoons poppy seeds

Curry powder 3

Madras-style – hot

IMPERIAL	METRIC	AMERICAN
1 oz. coriander seeds	25 g. coriander seeds	2½ tablespoons coriander seeds
2 teaspoons garlic powder	2 teaspoons garlic powder	2 teaspoons garlic powder
1 tablespoon ground cumin	1 tablespoon ground cumin	1 tablespoon ground cumin
2 teaspoons ground turmeric	2 teaspoons ground turmeric	2 teaspoons ground turmeric
1 teaspoon ground ginger	1 teaspoon ground ginger	1 teaspoon ground ginger
1 teaspoon chilli seasoning	1 teaspoon chilli seasoning	1 teaspoon chili seasoning
½ teaspoon ground allspice	½ teaspoon ground allspice	½ teaspoon ground allspice
1 tablespoon salt	1 tablespoon salt	1 tablespoon salt
1 tablespoon ground black pepper	1 tablespoon ground black pepper	1 tablespoon ground black pepper
½ tablespoon dry mustard	½ tablespoon dry mustard	½ tablespoon dry mustard
¼ teaspoon saffron	¼ teaspoon saffron	¼ teaspoon saffron

Grind coriander seeds (sieve if any large husks remain). Mix all ingredients together. Keep in an airtight jar. This recipe makes 3 oz. (80 g.) curry powder.

Curry powder 4

A good basic blend from ready-ground spices

IMPERIAL	METRIC	AMERICAN
3 tablespoons ground cinnamon	3 tablespoons ground cinnamon	¼ cup ground cinnamon
2 tablespoons ground coriander	2 tablespoons ground coriander	2½ tablespoons ground coriander
2 tablespoons ground turmeric	2 tablespoons ground turmeric	2½ tablespoons ground turmeric
2½ tablespoons ground cumin	2½ tablespoons ground cumin	3 tablespoons ground cumin
1 tablespoon ground fenugreek	1 tablespoon ground fenugreek	1 tablespoon ground fenugreek
1½ tablespoons dry mustard	1½ tablespoons dry mustard	2 tablespoons dry mustard
1½ tablespoons ground cardamom	1½ tablespoons ground cardamom	2 tablespoons ground cardamom
1½ tablespoons garlic salt	1½ tablespoons garlic salt	2 tablespoons garlic salt
1½ tablespoons ground poppy seeds	1½ tablespoons ground poppy seeds	2 tablespoons ground poppy seeds
2 tablespoons ground chillis	2 tablespoons ground chillis	2½ tablespoons ground dried chilis
2 tablespoons ground black pepper	2 tablespoons ground black pepper	2½ tablespoons ground black pepper
1 tablespoon ground ginger	1 tablespoon ground ginger	1 tablespoon ground ginger

Sprinkle often with vinegar while blending these spices. This powder may be sealed tightly and stored for many months, but it will not give the same rich flavour as powders using whole spices and freshly ground.

Garam masala

Although it can include some of the same spices that go into curry powder, it is not a curry powder. Unlike curry powder, it should be added at the end of cooking time so that its delicate flavour is retained. The spices used are variable. Garam masala can be obtained from shops selling Indian foodstuffs, but below are two recipes for your cupboard to be made at home and stored for use when required. After a time you might develop a taste for certain spices, and want to make additions or alter quantities to develop your own particular blend.

Garam masala 1

Cooking time: few minutes

IMPERIAL	METRIC	AMERICAN
8 oz. coriander seeds	225 g. coriander seeds	2½ cups coriander seeds
4 oz. cumin seeds	110 g. cumin seeds	1 cup cumin seeds
4 oz. large cardamoms	110 g. large cardamoms	¼ lb. large cardamoms
2 oz. cinnamon	50 g. cinnamon	½ cup cinnamon
2 oz. cloves	50 g. cloves	⅔ cup cloves
4 oz. peppercorns	110 g. peppercorns	1 cup peppercorns
1 teaspoon grated nutmeg	1 teaspoon grated nutmeg	1 teaspoon grated nutmeg

Roast the coriander and cumin seeds, separately, in a warm oven or under a low grill for about 3–5 minutes, shaking them round constantly if under a grill. This is to make them easier to grind, and seeds should not burn.

Peel the cardamoms. Remove husks and strawy bits. Grind all the spices in a blender or finely adjusted coffee grinder. Store in an airtight container. Use as directed in recipes.

Garam masala 2

IMPERIAL	METRIC	AMERICAN
6 tablespoons black pepper	6 tablespoons black pepper	½ cup black pepper
5 tablespoons dark caraway seeds	5 tablespoons dark caraway seeds	6 tablespoons dark caraway seeds
2 tablespoons ground cinnamon	2 tablespoons ground cinnamon	2½ tablespoons ground cinnamon
6 tablespoons coriander	6 tablespoons coriander	½ cup coriander
2 tablespoons ground cloves	2 tablespoons ground cloves	2½ tablespoons ground cloves
1½ tablespoons cardamom seeds	1½ tablespoons cardamom seeds	2 tablespoons cardamom seeds

Pick over the ingredients and remove any husks, or strawy bits. Grind together in a blender or in a finely adjusted coffee grinder. Do not make the mixture too fine. Store in an airtight container and keep for use. **Note**: this Garam masala is fragrant and strong. Its robust flavour goes well with meat, fried and braised foods. Try it sprinkled on fried potatoes, with a pinch of turmeric. Sprinkle a little on yogurt, sour cream and curd cheeses.

Curry paste

In some recipes curry paste is called for, either without, or sometimes with, curry powder. This can be bought in tins or jars, but better still, you can make your own curry pastes.

A Thai housewife takes the 'right' amounts of each spice without the help of a measuring spoon, and she pounds them together in a mortar with a pestle. If you do not have a pestle and mortar, a good pepper grinder does an efficient job on seeds of coriander, cardamom, and caraway. You should measure them, however, after they are ground as they tend to increase in bulk. After pounding, the Thais blend their spices with *kapi*, a paste made of shrimps, but you will find a mixture of anchovy paste and vinegar works almost as well.

When preparing curry, for each pound of meat use approximately 2 teaspoons curry paste and just under ½ pint (3 dl.) liquid (i.e. stock, coconut milk, or milk, etc.). And because both fish and fowl take less time to cook than meat, the liquid for these should be reduced by about half. Approximately half as much curry paste should be used, although this is a matter of taste.

You may prepare the paste in advance to have on hand when you need it. Stored in small jars in the refrigerator, it will keep for weeks.

Curry paste for meat

IMPERIAL	METRIC	AMERICAN
1 tablespoon freshly ground nutmeg	1 tablespoon freshly ground nutmeg	1 tablespoon freshly ground nutmeg
½ teaspoon ground cloves	½ teaspoon ground cloves	½ teaspoon ground cloves
1 teaspoon mace	1 teaspoon mace	1 teaspoon mace
10 cardamom pods (remove seeds to grind) *or* 1 teaspoon cardamom powder	10 cardamom pods (remove seeds to grind) *or* 1 teaspoon cardamom powder	10 cardamom pods (remove seeds to grind) *or* 1 teaspoon cardamom powder
¼ teaspoon cayenne pepper	¼ teaspoon cayenne pepper	¼ teaspoon cayenne pepper
2 tablespoons ground coriander	2 tablespoons ground coriander	2½ tablespoons ground coriander
½ teaspoon ground caraway	½ teaspoon ground caraway	½ teaspoon ground caraway
1½ teaspoons paprika	1½ teaspoons paprika	1½ teaspoons paprika
2 tablespoons anchovy paste	2 tablespoons anchovy paste	2½ tablespoons anchovy paste
2 teaspoons vinegar	2 teaspoons vinegar	2 teaspoons vinegar

Combine all dry ingredients. Add the anchovy paste and vinegar, mix. Keep in an airtight jar.

Curry paste for poultry and sea food

IMPERIAL	METRIC	AMERICAN
1 tablespoon ground coriander	1 tablespoon ground coriander	1 tablespoon ground coriander
1 tablespoon ground caraway	1 tablespoon ground caraway	1 tablespoon ground caraway
1 teaspoon ground turmeric	1 teaspoon ground turmeric	1 teaspoon ground turmeric
1 teaspoon ground black pepper	1 teaspoon ground black pepper	1 teaspoon ground black pepper
¼ teaspoon cayenne pepper	¼ teaspoon cayenne pepper	¼ teaspoon cayenne pepper
½ teaspoon freshly grated nutmeg	½ teaspoon freshly grated nutmeg	½ teaspoon freshly grated nutmeg
2 tablespoons anchovy paste	2 tablespoons anchovy paste	2½ tablespoons anchovy paste
2 teaspoons vinegar	2 teaspoons vinegar	2 teaspoons vinegar

Combine all dry ingredients. Add the anchovy paste and vinegar, mix. Keep in an airtight jar.

Other ingredients

All the ingredients mentioned in this book are widely available. If not at your local grocery store, there are a number of shops specializing in importing Indian foods where it is possible to get most ingredients for a curry meal. However, where difficulty is foreseen, substitutes are suggested.

Ghee. This is clarified butter made from buffalo milk, and it is imported in tins. Any butter, clarified, will do, or unclarified butter, although it is more apt to burn because of the milky particles still in it.

Butter can be clarified in the following way: place butter in saucepan, heat gently until bubbles form on the surface. Increase heat a little; skim foam from surface as it forms. Remove from heat, let it stand a few minutes so that the sediment will settle. Strain through fine muslin into a basin, leaving sediment behind in the saucepan.

Oil. Fat or oil used in cooking is just as important as the food cooked. All the different oils, coconut, olive, peanut (groundnut) and sesame give different flavours just as butter, lard or dripping do. Mustard oil, for instance, is always used in India for cooking fish. However, although most of these are obtainable, if you do not wish to stock a variety of cooking oils, use a good vegetable oil that does not have an obtrusive flavour.

Yogurt. Indians use yogurt in cooking as the French do wine. Yogurt has some remarkable properties for assimilating spices, removing any excessive pungency, and impregnating the food with the flavour of the ingredients used. Also, natural yogurt does not curdle or separate as cream does in cooking. Yogurt never obtrudes; it leaves no taste. It loses its own to intensify other flavours. There is no residue, fat, oil or sludge left from it.

Tamarind sauce or purée. Imported, and can be bought in jars or cans. But if not available, for each tablespoon of tamarind sauce called for in recipes, substitute 2 teaspoons of plum jam, combined with 2 teaspoons lemon juice.

Coconut cream. Available, packaged in blocks, from Oriental and gourmet food stores.

Coconut milk. This can be bought in cans, but it can be simply made with fresh coconut, or with desiccated coconut (see page 11).

Bombay duck. It is not a duck but a fried fish. In the West today, Bombay duck is perhaps the best known of all curry accompaniments. The fish is a small gelatinous creature known as the bummalo or bombil. It is found in the salt waters around India. When dried it is boxed up and sent abroad as an expensive delicacy. The dull, flat, rubbery looking fish is most unappetizing as it comes from the box. Since the disagreeable odour of crisped Bombay duck lingers, it should be prepared several hours in advance and kept in a dry place until just before the curry is served. Brown the fish quickly in a hot oven until they each begin to curl at the edge and turn golden brown. Take from the oven and let cool; as it cools it will curl and crisp within a minute or two. It is now an intriguing morsel waiting to be crumbled on top of curry. It is also used as an ingredient in curries and curry sauces.

How to eat curry

Indians are dexterous with their hands at eating curry. For Westerners, however, a fork and spoon are best – not just a fork.

When choosing from the delightful side dishes for curry – the sambals of chutney, relishes, etc. – put just a small quantity on the plate. Eat the sambals intermittently by taking a little of one, then another, mixing each with a spoonful of curry and rice. If you have a very hot chilli pickle, it is easy with a spoon and fork, to break off just a little of the chilli and mix it with a good quantity of rice – thus making a savoury mouthful, instead of a fiery one.

The blandness of rice cuts down the hotness of curries. If you have a curry that is too hot for your taste, mix it with a generous amount of rice. It will then be pleasantly palatable.

Desserts to serve after curry

You will not find recipes for desserts in this book, as it is strictly a book of curries. Oriental desserts tend to be very sweet, and do not often suit the Western palate.

A good fruit salad rounds off a curry meal for some, and if you want it to have a taste of the East, start it with a can of guavas or mango slices. Add sliced bananas, apples, grapes, blanched almonds, any other fruits in season, and tiny slivers of preserved ginger.

A more elaborate dish on this theme would be a Fruit salad Pavlova: fruit salad served in a meringue case. Pears poached in red wine with a cinnamon stick and sugar, and served with cream, or better still with chocolate sauce and cream, makes another special follow-up for curry. Alternatively, ice cream is always refreshing after curry.

Curry sauces

This is a small section, but there are sauces which are traditional and used in a variety of dishes, such as *korma*, others which are poured over rice, and those which are a useful standby for using up left-over vegetables and meat. Because coconut milk is so often the stock for a sauce, we examine what it is and how to make it.

Coconut milk for curries

A number of recipes you will find, especially ones from Southern India, Ceylon and Indonesia, use coconut milk as a stock. Before trying out these recipes it is important to understand what is meant by coconut milk. The liquid in the coconut we call milk is called 'water', and discarded in some places, used for drinking in others. To make the milk used in curries, remove the nut from its hard, fibrous shell, scrape off the brown, inner skin. Grate the coconut finely into a bowl, cover with ½ pint (3 dl.) boiling water, leave for 45 to 60 minutes. Strain off the liquid, put the coconut in a muslin bag, and squeeze to extract as much liquid as possible. This is called the *thick* or *first* milk. The same process is repeated but this time the strained coconut is soaked for 12 hours and then strained again. This is the *second* milk. The second milk is used for cooking the curry instead of stock or water, and the first, or thick milk, is stirred in at the last moment to give a bland, lovely flavour and texture to the curry.

Coconut milk can also be made from dried (unsweetened) coconut. Take 8 oz. (225 g., 3 cups) desiccated coconut, cover it with 1 pint (½ litre, 2½ cups) of boiling water, leave for 24 hours. Strain and use it in the same way as the milk made from freshly grated coconut. This can be substituted for both the thick and second milk mentioned in recipes, although it will not be as rich as the first milk made with fresh coconut.

A good curry sauce is a practical way of using up left-over meat and vegetables. Make the sauce, add the meat, and cook the mixture just long enough to heat through.

Curry sauce

Cooking time:
1 hour 15 minutes

IMPERIAL	METRIC	AMERICAN
1 apple	1 apple	1 apple
1 small onion	1 small onion	1 small onion
1 oz. butter	25 g. butter	2 tablespoons butter
1 oz. curry powder	25 g. curry powder	¼ cup curry powder
1 oz. flour	25 g. flour	¼ cup flour
¾ pint stock *or* water	scant ½ litre stock *or* water	2 cups stock *or* water
1 teaspoon lemon juice	1 teaspoon lemon juice	1 teaspoon lemon juice
¼ pint coconut milk	1½ dl. coconut milk	⅔ cup coconut milk
1 oz. sultanas	25 g. sultanas	3 tablespoons white raisins
1 tablespoon mango chutney	1 tablespoon mango chutney	1 tablespoon mango chutney
1 tablespoon freshly grated coconut	1 tablespoon freshly grated coconut	1 tablespoon freshly grated coconut

Prepare and chop apple and onion finely. Melt the butter and fry onion in it. Add curry powder and flour and fry until fat is absorbed. Add stock, bring sauce to the boil, skim well, then add all other ingredients except chutney and coconut. Simmer for 1 hour, then stir in chutney and grated coconut. Pour into a china or enamel basin; allow to stand overnight to mellow. Reheat when required.

Indonesian sate sauce

Cooking time: 10 minutes
Serves: 4–6

IMPERIAL	METRIC	AMERICAN
1–2 red chillis	1–2 red chillis	1–2 red chilis
2–3 garlic cloves, fried	2–3 garlic cloves, fried	2–3 garlic cloves, fried
4 tablespoons peanut butter	4 tablespoons peanut butter	⅓ cup peanut butter
½ chicken stock cube	½ chicken stock cube	½ chicken bouillon cube
4 tablespoons boiling water	4 tablespoons boiling water	⅓ cup boiling water
lemon juice	lemon juice	lemon juice

Mince or pound the chillis and garlic together, add the peanut butter and chicken cube dissolved in the boiling water, add lemon juice to taste. Cook over a low heat and stir until the sauce is smooth. Serve with skewered lamb or as a side dish for curry.

Korma

Cooking time: 1 hour

IMPERIAL	METRIC	AMERICAN
½ pint yogurt	3 dl. yogurt	1¼ cups yogurt
1 tablespoon minced green pepper	1 tablespoon minced green pepper	1 tablespoon minced green pepper
½ teaspoon ground ginger	½ teaspoon ground ginger	½ teaspoon ground ginger
1 teaspoon ground cinnamon	1 teaspoon ground cinnamon	1 teaspoon ground cinnamon
1 teaspoon ground turmeric	1 teaspoon ground turmeric	1 teaspoon ground turmeric
½ teaspoon freshly ground black pepper	½ teaspoon freshly ground black pepper	½ teaspoon freshly ground black pepper
2 teaspoons poppy seeds	2 teaspoons poppy seeds	2 teaspoons poppy seeds
2 teaspoons ground almonds	2 teaspoons ground almonds	2 teaspoons ground almonds
1 teaspoon salt	1 teaspoon salt	1 teaspoon salt

Mix all ingredients in the top part of a double boiler and simmer over boiling water for 1 hour, or until the mixture loses the raw spice taste. Seal the korma in a sterilized jar. It will keep for many weeks; to be used in pulao mixtures.

Sweet curry sauce

Cooking time: 45 minutes

IMPERIAL	METRIC	AMERICAN
1 medium onion	1 medium onion	1 medium onion
2 cooking apples	2 cooking apples	2 cooking apples
3 oz. butter	80 g. butter	6 tablespoons butter
1 teaspoon grated lemon rind	1 teaspoon grated lemon rind	1 teaspoon grated lemon rind
1 tablespoon raisins, chopped	1 tablespoon raisins, chopped	1 tablespoon raisins, chopped
2 tablespoons curry powder	2 tablespoons curry powder	2½ tablespoons curry powder
3 tablespoons flour	3 tablespoons flour	¼ cup flour
1 pint chicken stock	generous ½ litre chicken stock	2½ cups chicken stock
1 teaspoon brown sugar	1 teaspoon brown sugar	1 teaspoon brown sugar
2 tablespoons redcurrant jelly	2 tablespoons redcurrant jelly	2½ tablespoons red currant jelly
2 teaspoons lemon juice	2 teaspoons lemon juice	2 teaspoons lemon juice

Chop onion, peel, core and chop apples. Melt butter, cook onion until transparent but not brown. Add prepared apples, lemon rind, raisins and curry powder; cook 2 minutes. Blend flour to a smooth paste with a little water, and add; cook further 3 minutes, stirring all the time. Gradually pour in stock, add sugar and redcurrant jelly, cover and simmer for 30 minutes. Strain sauce through muslin, stir in lemon juice.

Curry soups

Every country has its favourite soups. The Russians pride themselves on their borshch, while the Americans go for chowders. The Spanish have gazpacho, the English their oxtail and pea soups, and the Scots their barley broth.

We have all heard of mulligatawny, and tasted some travesties of it, too. The real thing bears no comparison. Good soup requires good fresh vegetables, meat on the bone, and long slow cooking. This is exactly what mulligatawny gets. There are many variations, but they are most of them a meal in themselves, and are usually served with boiled rice to be added by the individual. Mulligatawny in its variety is covered in this chapter, as well as other more unusual curried soups, including several which are served cold.

Chicken mulligatawny

Cooking time: 4–5 hours
Serves: 6

IMPERIAL	METRIC	AMERICAN
1 boiling chicken (about 4 lb.)	1 boiling chicken (about 2 kg.)	1 stewing chicken (about 4 lb.)
3 pints water	1½ litres water	7½ cups water
2 teaspoons salt	2 teaspoons salt	2 teaspoons salt
8 tablespoons butter	8 tablespoons butter	$\frac{2}{3}$ cup butter
1 onion, minced	1 onion, minced	1 onion, minced
1 tablespoon curry powder	1 tablespoon curry powder	1 tablespoon curry powder
1 tablespoon flour	1 tablespoon flour	1 tablespoon flour
1 teaspoon sugar	1 teaspoon sugar	1 teaspoon sugar
2 unpeeled cooking apples, diced	2 unpeeled cooking apples, diced	2 unpeeled cooking apples, diced
2 green peppers, chopped	2 green peppers, chopped	2 green sweet peppers, chopped
4 oz. celery, chopped	110 g. celery, chopped	1 cup celery, chopped
2 carrots, finely chopped	2 carrots, finely chopped	2 carrots, finely chopped
2 cloves	2 cloves	2 cloves
1 teaspoon ground mace	1 teaspoon ground mace	1 teaspoon ground mace
½ teaspoon freshly ground black pepper	½ teaspoon freshly ground black pepper	½ teaspoon freshly ground black pepper
8 oz. tomato pulp	225 g. tomato pulp	½ lb. tomato pulp

Cut the chicken into pieces and put it into a heavy saucepan with the water and half the salt. Simmer for 3–4 hours, or until the meat is tender but still firm. Remove the chicken from the pan, take meat from the bones, and return the bones to the stock. Cut the chicken into small pieces and set aside. Cook the stock and bones until the liquid is reduced by about one-third. Discard bones and reserve 1½ pints (1 litre, 3¾ cups) liquid in saucepan.

Heat the butter in a frying pan and brown the chicken pieces; remove chicken, brown the onion, then remove onion. Fry the mixed curry powder and flour in the same pan. Add the sugar and simmer until a smooth paste is formed. Add to the reserved stock in saucepan with remaining salt, the apples, green peppers, celery, carrots, cloves, mace, and black pepper. Simmer the soup for 30 minutes, or until vegetables are soft. Force broth and vegetables through a sieve, or liquidize. Return the puréed mixture to the saucepan and add the chicken, browned onion, and tomato pulp. Simmer for 10 minutes longer. Serve hot boiled rice in a separate dish.

Mulligatawny soup

Cooking time:
1 hour 20 minutes
Serves: 4

IMPERIAL	METRIC	AMERICAN
8 whole peppercorns	8 whole peppercorns	8 whole peppercorns
bouquet garni of 1 bay leaf, parsley, sprig thyme	bouquet garni of 1 bay leaf, parsley, sprig thyme	bouquet garni of 1 bay leaf, parsley, sprig thyme
thinly peeled rind of $\frac{1}{2}$ lemon	thinly peeled rind of $\frac{1}{2}$ lemon	thinly peeled rind of $\frac{1}{2}$ lemon
$1\frac{1}{2}$ pints lightly coloured beef stock	scant 1 litre lightly coloured beef stock	$3\frac{3}{4}$ cups lightly colored beef stock
$\frac{1}{4}$ pint boiling water	$1\frac{1}{2}$ dl. boiling water	$\frac{2}{3}$ cup boiling water
2 tablespoons desiccated coconut	2 tablespoons desiccated coconut	3 tablespoons shredded coconut
1 medium onion	1 medium onion	1 medium onion
2 oz. butter	50 g. butter	$\frac{1}{4}$ cup butter
2 teaspoons curry powder	2 teaspoons curry powder	2 teaspoons curry powder
1 teaspoon curry paste	1 teaspoon curry paste	1 teaspoon curry paste
$1\frac{1}{2}$ oz. plain flour	40 g. plain flour	6 tablespoons all-purpose flour
$1\frac{1}{2}$ oz. dried milk	40 g. dried milk	$\frac{1}{2}$ cup dried milk solids
$\frac{3}{4}$ pint water	scant $\frac{1}{2}$ litre water	2 cups water
1 teaspoon lemon juice	1 teaspoon lemon juice	1 teaspoon lemon juice
salt and pepper	salt and pepper	salt and pepper
2 oz. cooked Patna rice	50 g. cooked Patna rice	$\frac{1}{3}$ cup cooked long grain rice
lemon wedges	lemon wedges	lemon wedges

Put the peppercorns, bouquet garni and lemon rind into a piece of muslin and tie into a bag. Slightly crush the spices to bruise them, then simmer in the stock for 30 minutes. Remove spice bag. Pour boiling water on to the coconut and set aside for half an hour. Peel and chop the onion finely; fry slowly in the butter until soft and pale brown. Stir in the curry powder, curry paste and lastly the flour. Cook for a few minutes then pour on the stock and the dried milk mixed with the $\frac{3}{4}$ pint water.

Strain the liquid from the coconut into the pan. Add lemon juice and adjust seasoning to taste. Bring to the boil and simmer for about 35 minutes. Sieve or liquidize soup and pour into bowls. Serve with rice floating on top and wedges of lemon.

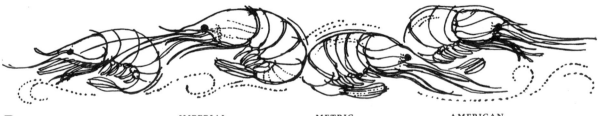

Prawn soup

Cooking time: 35 minutes
Serves: 4

IMPERIAL	METRIC	AMERICAN
4 tablespoons mustard oil *or* butter	4 tablespoons mustard oil *or* butter	$\frac{1}{3}$ cup mustard oil *or* butter
1 onion, minced	1 onion, minced	1 onion, minced
2 teaspoons curry powder	2 teaspoons curry powder	2 teaspoons curry powder
1 lb. peeled prawns	450 g. peeled prawns	1 lb. shelled prawns *or* shrimp
$1\frac{1}{2}$ pints water	scant 1 litre water	$3\frac{3}{4}$ cups water
1 teaspoon salt	1 teaspoon salt	1 teaspoon salt
$\frac{1}{2}$ pint coconut milk (see page 11)	3 dl. coconut milk (see page 11)	$1\frac{1}{4}$ cups coconut milk (see page 11)

Heat the oil or butter and brown the onion lightly in it; remove onion from pan. In remaining oil fry the curry powder to dark brown. Add the peeled prawns and simmer for 3 minutes. Return the browned onions to the pan and add water and salt. Bring to the boil. Cover and let simmer for 15 minutes or less, until the prawns are tender. Add the coconut milk and simmer for 5 minutes longer.

Cold curried soups

Cold soups have always been popular in hot lands and are gradually gaining favour in the West. These soups are prepared in the same way as hot soups, with the curry powder cooked beforehand to avoid any raw curry taste, and in keeping with the unfailing rule: curry powder must first be fried in fat before being added to any dish, hot or cold. An important advantage of these soups is that they can be cooked the day before required.

Curried apple soup

Cooking time: 30 minutes
Serves: 6

IMPERIAL	METRIC	AMERICAN
2 cooking apples	2 cooking apples	2 cooking apples
lemon juice	lemon juice	lemon juice
2 teaspoons curry powder	2 teaspoons curry powder	2 teaspoons curry powder
2 tablespoons butter *or* vegetable oil	2 tablespoons butter *or* vegetable oil	3 tablespoons butter *or* vegetable oil
2 pints chicken stock	generous 1 litre chicken stock	5 cups chicken stock
1 teaspoon salt	1 teaspoon salt	1 teaspoon salt
$\frac{1}{4}$ pint apple juice	$1\frac{1}{2}$ dl. apple juice	$\frac{2}{3}$ cup apple juice
$\frac{1}{2}$ pint thick cream	3 dl. thick cream	$1\frac{1}{4}$ cups whipping cream
ground ginger	ground ginger	ground ginger

Peel the apples and core them, keeping a few curls of peel for garnish. Mince this peel and keep it in water with a little lemon juice until needed. Fry the curry powder in the butter till dark brown. Stir in about a quarter of the stock and cook until the mixture is smooth. Add the rest of the stock and the salt. Mince the apples and drop immediately into the stock in order that they do not discolour in the air. Cover and allow to simmer gently for 20 minutes, or until apples are soft. Add the apple juice and blend well. Chill the soup for several hours. Add chilled cream just before serving. Sprinkle a little ginger on top, if liked, and garnish with the minced peel.

Curried broccoli soup

Cooking time: 30 minutes
Serves: 4

IMPERIAL	METRIC	AMERICAN
2 lb. broccoli	1 kg. broccoli	2 lb. broccoli
salt	salt	salt
$1\frac{1}{2}$ pints chicken stock	scant 1 litre chicken stock	$3\frac{3}{4}$ cups chicken stock
1 tablespoon butter *or* vegetable oil	1 tablespoon butter *or* vegetable oil	1 tablespoon butter *or* vegetable oil
1 onion, finely chopped	1 onion, finely chopped	1 onion, finely chopped
2 teaspoons curry powder	2 teaspoons curry powder	2 teaspoons curry powder
$\frac{1}{8}$ teaspoon cayenne pepper	$\frac{1}{8}$ teaspoon cayenne pepper	$\frac{1}{8}$ teaspoon cayenne pepper
1 tablespoon cornflour	1 tablespoon cornflour	1 tablespoon cornstarch
$\frac{1}{4}$ pint thick cream	$1\frac{1}{2}$ dl. thick cream	$\frac{2}{3}$ cup whipping cream
2 oz. fresh watercress, finely chopped	50 g. fresh watercress, finely chopped	$\frac{1}{2}$ cup finely chopped fresh watercress

Clean the broccoli and cut it into pieces. Cover with boiling water with 1 teaspoon salt added, and cook for about 15 minutes, until it is tender. Drain, mash, and add to chicken stock in a heavy saucepan. Heat butter in a separate pan and brown the onion lightly. Add onion to the stock.

In remaining butter in pan, fry the curry powder and cayenne to a dark brown. Stir in the cornflour and cook to a smooth paste. Add a little of the stock to this, mix well, and then return all to the saucepan. Allow to simmer for 5 minutes, then press all through a sieve. Add more salt to taste if needed. Chill well. Add the chilled cream just before serving. Sprinkle with chopped watercress.

Rice

Rice is native to India: almost 6,000 years ago it was already being cultivated there, from the wild grain found in the plains and in the Himalayas. Today it grows all over the world wherever the climate will permit, and more than half the world's population obtains its nourishment – about 80 per cent of its calories – from this grain.

Few other foods are as easy to assimilate and to digest. Contrary to general opinion the white milled grain of rice is not 'all starch, anyway'; it contains a high proportion of vegetable proteins. With today's milling of rice the starch content is in many cases reduced and then no washing is necessary. The milling is a cleaning process. Also, rice cooked in an open pan tends to lose food value if excess water is drained off after cooking. So, it is best to cook rice in the smallest amount of water: this ensures its best flavour and guards the nutrient within the grain.

Brown rice, or rice that has been merely hulled, has as much protein as whole wheat. It has a pleasant, nutty flavour, too, when cooked. There are many different kinds of rice available. There is polished rice, unpolished, pre-cooked, rice ready in a bag for cooking, long grain, short grain, and wild rice which is astronomically expensive and is not a rice at all, but a native North American grass. If you like Eastern dishes, you should find your nearest Indian or Oriental grocers' shop and ask their advice. The best available long or longest grain rice is most suitable for cooking with curries. Should you be lucky you might be able to buy some of an aged Indian rice – this can be as much as 15 years old and makes magnificent pulao dishes. However, if you are unable to get to a specialist shop, buy the very best Patna or Siam rice you can find.

Plain boiled rice

With so many different kinds of rice it is impossible to give one way of cooking that covers them all. The brown, unpolished rice, for instance, takes longer than any of the white varieties. If you use the quick-cook variety, follow the directions on the packet, and do not leave it a minute longer on the stove, for these pre-prepared grains really do cook quickly, and easily become a soggy mess. However, if you follow a few basic rules, there is no reason why you should not cook rice perfectly: rice that is fluffy and dry, without lumps or the grains clogging together.

1 The type of rice: for curries buy the best type of long grain rice available.

2 The vessel used for cooking: use a saucepan or casserole of heavy metal, and until you reach the stage where you can cook rice under any conditions, or in any pan, keep to the same pan and get to know its reaction to rice, water, heat and stirring.

3 Amount of water: measure this carefully according to the cooking method you adopt, and until you learn to judge it by sight.

4 The degree of heat for cooking: except for the short time at the beginning needed to boil the water, the heat used is always gentle.

5 Stirring: the only time you stir is when you first put the rice grains into the boiling water. Resist the impulse to stir in the final stages of cooking, for this can damage the grains and spoil the dry, fluffy appearance expected as an end result.

Here are some well-tried methods of cooking plain boiled rice. There is certain to be one of these, at least, that suits you. A couple of attempts with it should give you any confidence you need, and then it is worthwhile adopting it for future use.

Notes

When working out the quantity of rice required, remember that in cooking it expands to three times its weight.

For extra whiteness add lemon juice to the cooking water.

When you stir rice, and this is only in the early stages of cooking, use a fork and not a spoon. Do not take off the lid until the end of the prescribed cooking time to look at it.

Where necessary, rinse the cooked rice with hot water to separate grains and spread on a flat tray or large dish and place in a warm oven to keep hot. Processed or converted rice, which absorbs all the water, does not need rinsing.

Boiled rice: little water method 1

IMPERIAL	METRIC	AMERICAN
1 lb. rice	450 g. rice	2½ cups rice
2¼ pints water	scant 1¼ litres water	5½ cups water
1 teaspoon salt	1 teaspoon salt	1 teaspoon salt

Cooking time: 18–20 minutes
Serves: 4–6

Add the rice to the rapidly boiling water to which salt has been added; stir with a fork until water is boiling again. Cover saucepan, keep boiling for about 1 minute. Lower the heat to its lowest, and cook until done. This should be in about 16–18 minutes. Test a grain with fingers or teeth. If underdone, sprinkle a tablespoon of water on it, and leave to cook for 2 minutes more. When rice is tender, take it off heat, but keep covered. Let it stand for 5–10 minutes, then serve. This should give it time to absorb all the water.

Boiled rice: little water method 2

IMPERIAL	METRIC	AMERICAN
1¾ pints water	1 litre water	4¼ cups water
1 teaspoon salt	1 teaspoon salt	1 teaspoon salt
1 lb. rice	450 g. rice	2½ cups rice

Cooking time: 15 minutes
Serves: 4–6

Bring the water with salt to the boil, add rice, stir. When boiling again, cover well. A damp cloth, covering the pot under the lid, will ensure that no steam escapes. Simmer on a low heat. After 14 minutes remove to a cool place and let stand for 10 minutes. Then serve.

Boiled rice: more water method 1

IMPERIAL	METRIC	AMERICAN
4 pints water	2¼ litres water	10 cups water
1 teaspoon salt	1 teaspoon salt	1 teaspoon salt
1 lb. rice	450 g. rice	2½ cups rice

Cooking time: 18–20 minutes
Serves: 4–6

Bring water with salt to the boil. Add rice. Leave to boil until rice is done – about 18 minutes, but test. If tender, add ½ pint (3 dl.) cold water immediately, and strain the rice. Put in a warm covered dish and serve after one minute.

Boiled rice: more water method 2

IMPERIAL	METRIC	AMERICAN
1 lb. rice	450 g. rice	2½ cups rice
4 pints water, salt added to taste	2¼ litres water, salt added to taste	10 cups water, salt added to taste

Cooking time: 15 minutes
Serves: 4–6

Dribble the rice through the fingers slowly into a pan of fast-boiling water. Boil at a gallop, 10 minutes, or until the grains are just tender. Pour in a cup of cold water to stop the boiling. Drain rice through a sieve and put in a dry pan. Cover with a linen cloth and let it stand on a very low heat or in the oven with the door open until the rice is quite dry. Shake the pan occasionally. This method breaks the slow-boiling rule, but there are people who swear by it.

To reheat left-over boiled rice

If you have a small quantity of rice left over and wish to combine it with freshly cooked rice, add the left-over rice to the rice you are boiling 3 minutes before you remove it from the stove.

If you have a large quantity of rice to reheat, bring plenty of water to the boil, and keep boiling. Add the left-over rice to the water, stir once with a fork, and leave for 5–10 seconds. Drain; keep covered in a hot dish for ½ minute before serving.

Fried rice

Cooking time: 45 minutes
Serves: 4–8

IMPERIAL	METRIC	AMERICAN
1 lb. long grain rice	450 g. long grain rice	2½ cups long grain rice
2 teaspoons salt	2 teaspoons salt	2 teaspoons salt
2 pints boiling water	generous 1 litre boiling water	5 cups boiling water
4 tablespoons butter or vegetable oil	4 tablespoons butter or vegetable oil	⅓ cup butter or vegetable oil

Wash and drain the rice. Mix well with the salt until the grains appear glazed. Cover with the boiling water. Bring to the boil again and simmer for about 25 minutes, until all water is absorbed.

Heat the butter to bubbling, add rice and fry to a light brown. Dry in an uncovered pan in a very slow oven, 250°F., 130°C., Gas Mark ½, for about 10 minutes, until the grains are fluffy.

Indonesian yellow rice

Cooking time: 30 minutes
Serves: 4

IMPERIAL	METRIC	AMERICAN
3 tablespoons freshly grated coconut or desiccated coconut	3 tablespoons freshly grated coconut or desiccated coconut	¼ cup freshly grated coconut or unsweetened shredded coconut
1¼ pints water	¾ litre water	3 cups water
1 teaspoon turmeric	1 teaspoon turmeric	1 teaspoon turmeric
¼ teaspoon salt	¼ teaspoon salt	¼ teaspoon salt
1 stock cube	1 stock cube	1 bouillon cube
¼ pint water	1½ dl. water	⅔ cup water
1 lb. long grain rice	450 g. long grain rice	2½ cups long grain rice
strips of red pepper	strips of red pepper	strips of red pepper
fried onion rings	fried onion rings	fried onion rings
thin slices cucumber	thin slices cucumber	thin slices cucumber
strips of flat omelette (see page 62)	strips of flat omelette (see page 62)	strips of flat omelette (see page 62)

Soak coconut in the 1¼ pints water overnight. Strain the water from the coconut; bring to the boil. Add turmeric, salt, and stock cube dissolved in the ¼ pint water. Add rice to the liquid, cook slowly until all the liquid has been absorbed. If rice is not cooked, add more liquid and continue cooking slowly until done. Decorate with the pepper, onion rings, cucumber and omelette strips.

Pulao rice

Cooking time: 45 minutes
Serves: 4

IMPERIAL	METRIC	AMERICAN
8 oz. long grain rice	225 g. long grain rice	1¼ cups long grain rice
2 oz. ghee or butter	50 g. ghee or butter	¼ cup ghee or butter
2 onions, sliced	2 onions, sliced	2 onions, sliced
1 garlic clove, crushed	1 garlic clove, crushed	1 garlic clove, crushed
1½ teaspoons salt	1½ teaspoons salt	1½ teaspoons salt
8 oz. peas	225 g. peas	1½ cups peas
1 pint hot water	generous ½ litre hot water	2½ cups hot water

Clean, wash and soak rice for half an hour. Heat ghee, fry onions until golden. Add drained rice, garlic, salt, and peas; continue to cook for 5 minutes, stirring. Gradually add hot water, mix thoroughly, and bring to the boil. Simmer, covered, 20 to 25 minutes, or until all liquid has been absorbed and rice is tender. **Note.** Any of the following can also be added: cloves, cinnamon, caraway seeds, turmeric, ginger, red pepper, coriander, parsley, garam masala or cumin.

Prawn curry with saffron rice (see recipe on page 28)

Pulao for stuffing chicken

Cooking time: 25 minutes
Makes: about 1½ lb. (700 g.)

IMPERIAL	METRIC	AMERICAN
4 tablespoons butter or vegetable oil	4 tablespoons butter or vegetable oil	⅓ cup butter or vegetable oil
1 onion, grated	1 onion, grated	1 onion, grated
1 teaspoon curry powder	1 teaspoon curry powder	1 teaspoon curry powder
1 garlic clove, crushed	1 garlic clove, crushed	1 garlic clove, crushed
¾ pint chicken stock	½ litre chicken stock	2 cups chicken stock
½ pint pineapple juice	3 dl. pineapple juice	1¼ cups pineapple juice
4 tablespoons raisins	4 tablespoons raisins	⅓ cup raisins
4 tablespoons pistachio nuts, chopped	4 tablespoons pistachio nuts, chopped	⅓ cup chopped pistachio nuts
12 oz. long grain rice	350 g. long grain rice	1¾ cups long grain rice
1 teaspoon salt	1 teaspoon salt	1 teaspoon salt

Heat the butter in a heavy pan and brown the onion in it; remove onion. Fry the curry powder until dark brown, add garlic and simmer for 3 minutes, until a smooth paste is formed. Return onion to the pan and add stock, pineapple juice, raisins, pistachios, and rice. Season with salt to taste. Cover tightly and simmer over low heat for 15 minutes, until rice is half done. Strain off liquid; reserve it for other uses. Use the pulao to stuff chickens or other poultry (enough for 1 large or 2 smaller chickens).

Red rice (West Indies)

Cooking time: 35 minutes
Serves: 4

IMPERIAL	METRIC	AMERICAN
1 lb. rice	450 g. rice	2½ cups rice
2 onions, chopped	2 onions, chopped	2 onions, chopped
oil for frying	oil for frying	oil for frying
salt to taste	salt to taste	salt to taste
4-oz. can tomato purée	110 g. tomato purée	½ cup tomato paste
2 tablespoons water	2 tablespoons water	3 tablespoons water
8 bacon rashers	8 bacon rashers	8 bacon slices

Boil the rice, drain and dry (see page 17). Sauté the onions with salt, add tomato purée, the water, then fold in the rice and turn gently for about five minutes. In the meantime, grill the bacon, cut it into pieces and serve on top of the red rice.

Saffron rice

Cooking time: 30 minutes
Serves: 4–6

IMPERIAL	METRIC	AMERICAN
1 oz. butter	50 g. butter	2 tablespoons butter
1 onion, finely chopped	1 onion, finely chopped	1 onion, finely chopped
1 lb. long grain rice	450 g. long grain rice	2½ cups long grain rice
½ teaspoon saffron	½ teaspoon saffron	½ teaspoon saffron
1½ pints hot chicken stock	scant 1 litre hot chicken stock	3¾ cups hot chicken stock

Heat butter in a large saucepan and sauté onion until golden. Add well-rinsed rice, stir over heat until rice is coated with butter. Add saffron to the hot chicken stock. Pour gradually into saucepan, stirring constantly. Bring to boil, then reduce heat, and cook slowly, covered, for 16 to 18 minutes until stock has been absorbed and rice is tender.

Savoury rice

Cooking time: 25 minutes
Serves: 4

IMPERIAL	METRIC	AMERICAN
butter for frying	butter for frying	butter for frying
2 leeks, chopped	2 leeks, chopped	2 leeks, chopped
1 green pepper, seeded and chopped	1 green pepper, seeded and chopped	1 green sweet pepper, seeded and chopped
1 small onion, chopped	1 small onion, chopped	1 small onion, chopped
4 eggs	4 eggs	4 eggs
salt and pepper	salt and pepper	salt and pepper
8 oz. cooked rice	225 g. cooked rice	1½ cups cooked rice

Heat the butter, fry the leeks, pepper and onion until they have softened but not browned. Beat the eggs, season to taste with salt and pepper, add to leeks and onions. Cook, stirring so the eggs are scrambled, then add cooked rice gradually, mixing well. Serve hot with curry or alone.

Burmese coconut rice

Cooking time: 40 minutes
Serves: 6–10

IMPERIAL	METRIC	AMERICAN
1½ pints milk	scant 1 litre milk	3¾ cups milk
1 lb. fresh shredded coconut	450 g. fresh shredded coconut	1 lb. fresh shredded coconut
1½ lb. long grain rice	700 g. long grain rice	3½ cups long grain rice
3 onions, grated	3 onions, grated	3 onions, grated
2 tablespoons peanut oil	2 tablespoons peanut oil	3 tablespoons peanut oil
½ teaspoon salt	½ teaspoon salt	½ teaspoon salt
½ pint extra coconut milk (see page 11)	3 dl. extra coconut milk (see page 11)	1¼ cups extra coconut milk (see page 11)

Bring the milk to the boil and add the shredded coconut. Remove from the heat at once and let stand, covered, for 1 hour. Mix the rice and onions and fry together in the heated oil for about 3 minutes. Add this mixture to the milk and coconut and add the salt. Mix well and bring to the boil. Reduce heat, cover, and let simmer over low heat for 30 minutes, or until rice has absorbed all the liquid. If mixture becomes too dry before rice is soft, add a little of the extra coconut milk; heat it before adding, but do not let it boil.

Simple sweet pulao

Cooking time: 35 minutes
Serves: 6

IMPERIAL	METRIC	AMERICAN
4 tablespoons butter	4 tablespoons butter	⅓ cup butter
1 lb. rice	450 g. rice	2½ cups rice
seeds of 3 cardamoms	seeds of 3 cardamoms	seeds of 3 cardamoms
6 cloves	6 cloves	6 cloves
4 oz. raisins	110 g. raisins	¾ cup raisins
4 oz. blanched almonds	110 g. blanched almonds	¾ cup blanched almonds
1½ tablespoons sugar	1½ tablespoons sugar	2 tablespoons sugar
2 blades mace	2 blades mace	2 blades mace
pinch salt	pinch salt	pinch salt
good pinch saffron	good pinch saffron	good pinch saffron
4-inch cinnamon stick	10-cm. cinnamon stick	4-inch cinnamon stick

Melt the butter and add the rice; brown it well without scorching it. Add the cardamom seeds, cloves, raisins, almonds, sugar, mace, salt and saffron. Stir in the pan for 1 minute. Cover with water, add the cinnamon, bring to the boil. Boil for 1 minute, then lower heat to simmer very gently in covered saucepan. Cook until rice is tender, adding water a little at a time, should liquid become absorbed before rice is cooked.

Breads

Bread and rice are seldom served together in curry-eating countries, but with many curries instead of rice a great variety of breads is eaten, especially in areas where wheat is grown or rice is scarce.

The bread served is usually flat and unleavened, but it has many variations. The simplest to make is called *chapati*. Chapati is made of wholemeal flours, mixed with water or water and milk. The rolled out dough is cooked quickly on a hot griddle. The thicker and more coarse of these is called *roti*, while the refined variety, light and thin in texture are known as *chapatis*. The lighter and larger the chapati, the more appreciated the cook.

Other forms of bread include: *parathas* made in much the same way as chapatis, but after the dough is rolled out ready for the griddle, the individual rounds are brushed with melted butter, and then fried. Parathas are often served stuffed. *Puris* are deep fried, and puffed and light.

Poppadums are paper-thin biscuits made from potato and lentil flour. Some are plain, others flavoured as spicy appetisers.

There are other kinds of flat breads, but only the more usual varieties are represented here. All these breads are served piping hot.

1. *Dividing chapati dough into portions.*

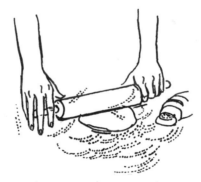

2. *Rolling out into thin pancakes.*

3. *Turning chapati to cook each side.*

Chapatis

(illustrated opposite)

Cooking time: 2 minutes each
Makes: 12

IMPERIAL	METRIC	AMERICAN
8 oz. wholemeal flour	225 g. wholemeal flour	2 cups whole wheat flour
1 teaspoon salt	1 teaspoon salt	1 teaspoon salt
$\frac{1}{4}$ pint water	$1\frac{1}{2}$ dl. water	$\frac{2}{3}$ cup water

Put flour and salt into basin. Add water and mix to a stiff dough: knead well until dough feels firm and elastic. Then place in a greased plastic bag, or in greaseproof paper, and leave in a warm place for 30 minutes. Turn on to a floured board, shape dough into a long roll, and divide into 12 equal slices. Roll out paper thin. Heat the heavy frying pan and, when *very* hot, cook chapatis for not more than one minute on either side. Cool in a tea towel.

Chapatis should always be cooked fresh for each meal.

To cook them: you can use an ungreased, heavy frying pan, griddle, bakestone or solid plate.
Left-over chapatis make an attractive crispbread when dried off in a cool oven.

Various breads: puris, chapatis and parathas (see recipes opposite, 24 and 25)

Malayan bread

Cooking time: 10–12 minutes
Makes: 4–5

IMPERIAL	METRIC	AMERICAN
8 oz. flour	225 g. flour	2 cups flour
1 teaspoon salt	1 teaspoon salt	1 teaspoon salt
1 egg, beaten	1 egg, beaten	1 egg, beaten
water for mixing	water for mixing	water for mixing
melted mutton fat	melted mutton fat	melted mutton fat

Sieve flour and salt on to a pastry board or table. Make a hollow in the centre and pour in beaten egg. Add a little cold water and mix to a stiff dough. Knead for several minutes. Divide dough into 3 pieces, roll each out very thinly. Spread dough with melted mutton fat. Pull the dough out by hand until it is paper thin. Gather up outside ends and knead all together again. Roll to a very long thin strip. Gather dough up at one end and roll the strip up. Roll it out thinly and cut out circles 6 inches (15 cm.) diameter. Heat fat in frying pan and fry the bread on both sides.

Parathas

(illustrated on page 23)

Cooking time: 2–3 minutes each
Makes: 12–16

IMPERIAL	METRIC	AMERICAN
2 lb. wholemeal flour	1 kg. wholemeal flour	8 cups whole wheat flour
3 teaspoons salt	3 teaspoons salt	3 teaspoons salt
about $\frac{3}{4}$ pint water	about $\frac{1}{2}$ litre water	about 2 cups water
$4\frac{1}{2}$ tablespoons butter	$4\frac{1}{2}$ tablespoons butter	$\frac{1}{3}$ cup butter

Sift flour and salt, and gradually add water, smoothing out any lumps, and making a pliable dough. Knead the dough well. Then cover it with a damp cloth and allow to stand for 1–1½ hours. Make small balls out of the dough. Roll them out thin and even. Then with the back of a tablespoon rub each pancake with melted butter. Fold once, and rub with more butter. Repeat once, better still, twice. Then roll them out again in triangle shapes. Heat the griddle and butter it slightly. Cook parathas on both sides, turning once. When finished, the bread is of a mild honey colour, and crisp. To make them crisper, substitute some of the water with about 4 tablespoons milk.

Stuffed parathas

Cooking time: 25 minutes plus
2–3 minutes each paratha
Makes: 12–16

IMPERIAL	METRIC	AMERICAN
3 medium potatoes	3 medium potatoes	3 medium potatoes
$4\frac{1}{2}$ tablespoons butter	$4\frac{1}{2}$ tablespoons butter	$\frac{1}{3}$ cup butter
2 onions, finely chopped	2 onions, finely chopped	2 onions, finely chopped
$\frac{1}{4}$ teaspoon ground ginger	$\frac{1}{4}$ teaspoon ground ginger	$\frac{1}{4}$ teaspoon ground ginger
$1\frac{1}{2}$ tablespoons mixed, chopped parsley, mint	$1\frac{1}{2}$ tablespoons mixed, chopped parsley, mint	2 tablespoons mixed, chopped parsley, mint
salt	salt	salt
2 tablespoons lemon juice	2 tablespoons lemon juice	3 tablespoons lemon juice
2 tablespoons chilli powder	2 tablespoons chilli powder	3 tablespoons chili powder
2 lb. wholemeal flour	1 kg. wholemeal flour	8 cups whole wheat flour
1 teaspoon salt	1 teaspoon salt	1 teaspoon salt
about $\frac{3}{4}$ pint water	about $\frac{1}{2}$ litre water	about 2 cups water

Boil the potatoes until tender, remove skin and mash. Heat a little of the butter and fry the onions with the ginger until transparent. Add the herbs, salt to taste, lemon juice and chilli. Mix in well with the potato and set aside. Make dough with flour, salt and water, as for Parathas above. Take each ball of dough, flatten and roll it out. Rub it with butter and place on it a tablespoon of the potato mixture. Fold it round and roll it out again. Cook on both sides on a heavy, buttered griddle until crisp and evenly golden.

Puris

(illustrated on page 23)

Cooking time: 40 minutes
Makes: 16

IMPERIAL	METRIC	AMERICAN
4 oz. plain flour	110 g. plain flour	1 cup all-purpose flour
4 oz. plain wheatmeal flour, finely ground	110 g. plain wheatmeal flour, finely ground	1 cup whole wheat flour
¼ pint water	1½ dl. water	⅔ cup water
1 teaspoon melted butter *or* ghee	1 teaspoon melted butter *or* ghee	1 teaspoon melted butter *or* ghee
2 teaspoons oil	2 teaspoons oil	2 teaspoons oil
ghee *or* oil for deep frying	ghee *or* oil for deep frying	ghee *or* oil for deep frying

Place flours in a bowl, add enough of the water to make a soft pliable dough. Add melted butter, knead until smooth. Cover bowl with a damp cloth, leave in warm place for one hour. Divide into 16 pieces and, using a little oil on the hands, shape into balls.

Grease rolling pin and board with oil, roll each ball into a thin pancake. Heat ghee until smoking hot, place a puri in frying pan. Turn immediately and press with a fish slice until the puri puffs up. Cook until golden. Drain on absorbent paper; serve as soon as possible.

Frying poppadums; hold flat in pan.

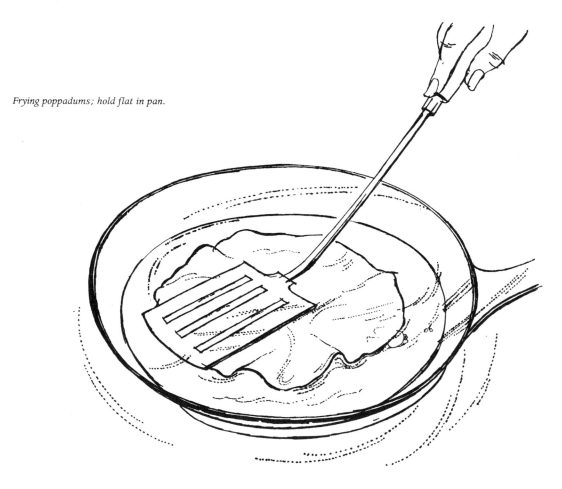

Poppadums

Poppadums are savoury lentil biscuits. They are difficult to make at home, but they can be bought in packaged form ready to cook.

They cook in a few seconds. Drop them one at a time into hot oil; they will puff up almost at once. Drain well on absorbent paper. They should be crisp and dry, not greasy to touch. If necessary, dry them off, when cooked, in a slow oven.

Fish curries

Fish forms the main part of the diet of most people living in the coastal regions of the Far East. The fish in these tropical waters are as strange and as exotic as are the fruits on the land. There are some 1,800 varieties ranging from giant deep-sea sharks to the tiny shrimps that teem in the waters of the paddy fields.

The curries in this section are concerned with a more limited collection of fish, but many of the recipes can be adapted to other kinds of fish, including some canned varieties.

Curried fillets of sole

(illustrated opposite)

Cooking time: 35 minutes
Serves: 5–10

IMPERIAL	METRIC	AMERICAN
4 tablespoons mustard oil *or* butter	4 tablespoons mustard oil *or* butter	$\frac{1}{3}$ cup mustard oil *or* butter
1 small onion, finely chopped	1 small onion, finely chopped	1 small onion, finely chopped
1 tablespoon curry powder	1 tablespoon curry powder	1 tablespoon curry powder
$\frac{3}{4}$ pint clear stock	$\frac{1}{2}$ litre clear stock	2 cups clear stock
1 teaspoon salt	1 teaspoon salt	1 teaspoon salt
10 fillets of sole *or* similar fish	10 fillets of sole *or* similar fish	10 fillets of sole *or* similar fish
juice of 1 lemon	juice of 1 lemon	juice of 1 lemon

Heat the oil in a heavy pan. Brown the onion lightly and remove it. In remaining oil fry the curry powder to a dark brown. Add the stock, the browned onion, and salt, and simmer for 5 minutes. Place the fillets in the pan so they are covered with the liquid. Simmer for 20 minutes or until fish is white and cooked firm but not mushy, and only a dribble of the liquid is left. Arrange fillets on a dish and mix remaining liquid with the lemon juice at the last minute, pouring over the fillets before serving.

Prawns in creamy curry sauce

Cooking time: 20 minutes
Serves: 4–6

IMPERIAL	METRIC	AMERICAN
2 oz. butter	50 g. butter	$\frac{1}{4}$ cup butter
2 teaspoons curry powder	2 teaspoons curry powder	2 teaspoons curry powder
1 tablespoon flour	1 tablespoon flour	1 tablespoon flour
$\frac{1}{4}$ teaspoon salt	$\frac{1}{4}$ teaspoon salt	$\frac{1}{4}$ teaspoon salt
$\frac{1}{4}$ teaspoon white pepper	$\frac{1}{4}$ teaspoon white pepper	$\frac{1}{4}$ teaspoon white pepper
$\frac{1}{2}$ pint milk	3 dl. milk	$1\frac{1}{4}$ cups milk
1 pint peeled prawns	generous $\frac{1}{2}$ litre peeled prawns	$2\frac{1}{2}$ cups shelled prawns or shrimp

Melt butter; stir in curry powder. Cook over a low heat, stirring, 2 to 3 minutes. Add flour, salt and pepper. Mix until well blended and smooth. Cook until bubbly, stirring constantly. Slowly stir in milk. Cook until thickened, continuing to stir, then add prawns. Heat them through. Serve over rice.

Curried fillets of sole (see recipe opposite)

Beef curry favourite (see recipe on page 35)

Prawn curry with saffron rice

(illustrated on page 19)

Cooking time: 30 minutes
Serves: 4

IMPERIAL	METRIC	AMERICAN
4 large onions	4 large onions	4 large onions
2 tablespoons oil	2 tablespoons oil	3 tablespoons oil
2 oz. haricot beans, soaked	50 g. haricot beans, soaked	¼ cup soaked navy beans
1 teaspoon ground ginger	1 teaspoon ground ginger	1 teaspoon ground ginger
1 tablespoon garlic powder	1 tablespoon garlic powder	1 tablespoon garlic powder
¼ teaspoon chilli seasoning	¼ teaspoon chilli seasoning	¼ teaspoon chili seasoning
½ teaspoon turmeric	½ teaspoon turmeric	½ teaspoon turmeric
½ pint water	3 dl. water	1¼ cups water
1 tablespoon tomato purée	1 tablespoon tomato purée	1 tablespoon tomato paste
1 lb. peeled prawns	450 g. peeled prawns	1 lb. shelled prawns or shrimp
1 dessert apple	1 dessert apple	1 eating apple
salt and pepper	salt and pepper	salt and pepper

Slice onions, then fry in oil until golden brown in a large heatproof casserole dish. Add soaked beans, ginger powder, garlic, chilli seasoning and turmeric. Cook for a further 10 minutes, stirring continuously.

Add water, tomato purée, prawns and peeled apple, cut into chunks. Simmer 10 minutes. Season to taste. Serve with saffron rice.

Goanese curried fish

Cooking time: 45 minutes
Serves: 2–3

IMPERIAL	METRIC	AMERICAN
1 lb. fish fillets	450 g. fish fillets	1 lb. fish fillets
pinch salt	pinch salt	pinch salt
2 tablespoons vinegar	2 tablespoons vinegar	3 tablespoons vinegar
pinch saffron	pinch saffron	pinch saffron
½ teaspoon peppercorns	½ teaspoon peppercorns	½ teaspoon peppercorns
1 teaspoon dry mustard	1 teaspoon dry mustard	1 teaspoon dry mustard
2 oz. ghee *or* 2 tablespoons vegetable oil	50 g. ghee *or* 2 tablespoons vegetable oil	¼ cup ghee *or* 3 tablespoons vegetable oil
1 large onion, finely sliced	1 large onion, finely sliced	1 large onion, finely sliced
2 garlic cloves, crushed	2 garlic cloves, crushed	2 garlic cloves, crushed
2 red chillis, finely chopped	2 red chillis, finely chopped	2 red chilis, finely chopped

Put the fish in an open pan, add salt and vinegar. Cook the saffron, peppercorns and mustard in the heated ghee or oil until well mixed. Pour this spice mixture over the fish in vinegar and cook gently for 15 minutes. Add the onion, garlic and chillis with about 4 tablespoons of water. Cook with a lid on, slowly, for 25 minutes.

Malayan lobster curry

Cooking time: 50 minutes
Serves: 4

IMPERIAL	METRIC	AMERICAN
1 cucumber	1 cucumber	1 cucumber
1 lb. lobster meat	450 g. lobster meat	1 lb. lobster meat
4 oz. ghee *or* butter	110 g. ghee *or* butter	½ cup ghee *or* butter
5 onions, chopped	5 onions, chopped	5 onions, chopped
2 garlic cloves, crushed	2 garlic cloves, crushed	2 garlic cloves, crushed
2 teaspoons ground ginger	2 teaspoons ground ginger	2 teaspoons ground ginger
pinch cayenne	pinch cayenne	pinch cayenne
2 teaspoons salt	2 teaspoons salt	2 teaspoons salt
2 tablespoons curry powder	2 tablespoons curry powder	3 tablespoons curry powder
2 tomatoes, chopped	2 tomatoes, chopped	2 tomatoes, chopped
2 tablespoons flour	2 tablespoons flour	3 tablespoons flour
1¼ pints coconut milk (see page 11)	¾ litre coconut milk (see page 11)	3 cups coconut milk (see page 11)
1 tablespoon lemon juice	1 tablespoon lemon juice	1 tablespoon lemon juice
2 teaspoons plum jam	2 teaspoons plum jam	2 teaspoons plum jam

Peel and cube the cucumber; cube the lobster meat. Heat butter, sauté onions and garlic 10 minutes. Add ginger, cayenne, salt, curry powder, and tomatoes. Cover, cook over a low heat 10 minutes, stirring frequently. Stir in the flour, and add coconut milk slowly. Continue to stir until boiling, then simmer 2 minutes. Add cucumber and lobster, cook over low heat 15 minutes. Combine lemon juice and jam, and add, mixing well. Serve hot with boiled rice.

Burmese prawn and bamboo shoot curry

Cooking time: 35 minutes
Serves: 4–6

IMPERIAL	METRIC	AMERICAN
3 tablespoons oil	3 tablespoons oil	¼ cup oil
4 onions, sliced	4 onions, sliced	4 onions, sliced
2 teaspoons turmeric	2 teaspoons turmeric	2 teaspoons turmeric
¼ teaspoon chilli powder	¼ teaspoon chilli powder	¼ teaspoon chili powder
boiling water	boiling water	boiling water
2 tablespoons finely chopped onion	2 tablespoons finely chopped onion	3 tablespoons finely chopped onion
2 garlic cloves	2 garlic cloves	2 garlic cloves
2 tablespoons finely chopped green ginger	2 tablespoons finely chopped green ginger	3 tablespoons finely chopped green ginger
2 lb. prawns	900 g. prawns	2 lb. prawns or shrimp
¾ pint coconut milk (see page 11)	scant ½ litre coconut milk (see page 11)	2 cups coconut milk (see page 11)
1 small can bamboo shoots	1 small can bamboo shoots	1 small can bamboo shoots
salt	salt	salt

Heat oil, fry sliced onions until they are golden. Add turmeric, chilli powder, and 1 tablespoon boiling water. Simmer a few minutes, then add finely chopped onion, crushed garlic, ginger, and 1 table-spoon boiling water. Continue to cook until oil rises to surface. Shell prawns. Add prawns, coconut milk, drained bamboo shoots; heat gently. Season to taste with salt.

Ceylonese prawn and tomato curry

(illustrated opposite)

Cooking time: 35 minutes
Serves: 4

IMPERIAL	METRIC	AMERICAN
1 tablespoon oil	1 tablespoon oil	1 tablespoon oil
1 small onion, chopped	1 small onion, chopped	1 small onion, chopped
2 lb. tomatoes	1 kg. tomatoes	2 lb. tomatoes
1 tablespoon tamarind purée *or* sauce (see page 10)	1 tablespoon tamarind purée *or* sauce (see page 10)	1 tablespoon tamarind purée *or* sauce (see page 10)
½ teaspoon chilli powder	½ teaspoon chilli powder	½ teaspoon chili powder
½ teaspoon turmeric	½ teaspoon turmeric	½ teaspoon turmeric
½-inch piece green ginger, sliced (see note)	1-cm. piece green ginger, sliced (see note)	½-inch piece green ginger, sliced (see note)
1¼ pints coconut milk (see page 11)	¾ litre coconut milk (see page 11)	3 cups coconut milk (see page 11)
3 garlic cloves, chopped	3 garlic cloves, chopped	3 garlic cloves, chopped
1½ lb. prawns	700 g. prawns	1½ lb. prawns *or* shrimp

Heat oil in saucepan, fry onion until golden. Peel and chop tomatoes, add to pan with remaining ingredients except prawns. Simmer, uncovered, until sauce has reached a fairly thick consistency. Shell and add prawns, stir over gentle heat until warmed through.

Crisply fried onion may be sprinkled on top before serving.
Note. Green ginger root must first be soaked in hot water for at least an hour, then scraped or peeled before slicing or cutting in chunks.

Crab curry (Ceylon)

Cooking time: 30 minutes
Serves: 2

IMPERIAL	METRIC	AMERICAN
meat from 1 large cooked crab *or* 1 large can crab	meat from 1 large cooked crab *or* 1 large can crab	meat from 1 large cooked crab *or* 1 large can crab
4 tablespoons second coconut milk (see page 11)	4 tablespoons second coconut milk (see page 11)	⅓ cup second coconut milk (see page 11)
10 ground chillis	10 ground chillis	10 ground chilis
1 small onion, chopped	1 small onion, chopped	1 small onion, chopped
4 garlic cloves, chopped	4 garlic cloves, chopped	4 garlic cloves, chopped
1 piece stem ginger, chopped	1 piece stem ginger, chopped	1 piece stem ginger, chopped
1-inch piece cinnamon *or* ½ teaspoon ground cinnamon	2·5-cm. piece cinnamon *or* ½ teaspoon ground cinnamon	1-inch piece cinnamon *or* ½ teaspoon ground cinnamon
salt	salt	salt
¾ pint thick coconut milk (see page 11)	scant ½ litre thick coconut milk (see page 11)	2 cups thick coconut milk (see page 11)
2 tablespoons desiccated *or* fresh grated coconut	2 tablespoons desiccated *or* fresh grated coconut	3 tablespoons shredded *or* fresh grated coconut
1 teaspoon uncooked rice	1 teaspoon uncooked rice	1 teaspoon uncooked rice
juice of 2 limes *or* lemons	juice of 2 limes *or* lemons	juice of 2 limes *or* lemons

If using canned crab break it up with a fork. Put the crab in a saucepan with the second milk, the chillis, onion, garlic, ginger, cinnamon and salt.

Cook until all the liquid is absorbed. Now add the thick milk, coconut, rice and lime juice. Simmer slowly until rice is tender. Serve hot.

Ceylonese prawn and tomato curry (see recipe opposite)

Southern prawn curry

Cooking time: 45 minutes
Serves: 4

IMPERIAL	METRIC	AMERICAN
1 oz. dried milk	25 g. dried milk	⅓ cup dried milk solids
1 pint water	generous ½ litre water	2½ cups water
2 oz. desiccated coconut	50 g. desiccated coconut	⅔ cup shredded coconut
2 oz. butter	50 g. butter	¼ cup butter
4 onions, chopped	4 onions, chopped	4 onions, chopped
4 garlic cloves, chopped	4 garlic cloves, chopped	4 garlic cloves, chopped
1½ oz. instant potato	40 g. instant potato	⅓ cup dry instant potato
1 teaspoon ground turmeric	1 teaspoon ground turmeric	1 teaspoon ground turmeric
4 dried chillis, crushed	4 dried chillis, crushed	4 dried chilis, crushed
2 teaspoons curry powder	2 teaspoons curry powder	2 teaspoons curry powder
1 teaspoon ground ginger	1 teaspoon ground ginger	1 teaspoon ground ginger
1 teaspoon lemon juice	1 teaspoon lemon juice	1 teaspoon lemon juice
1 lb. peeled prawns	450 g. peeled prawns	1 lb. shelled prawns *or* shrimp
1 teaspoon salt	1 teaspoon salt	1 teaspoon salt
lemon wedges	lemon wedges	lemon wedges

Dissolve the milk powder in the water, and warm. Pour this liquid over the coconut and leave to stand for an hour. Melt the butter in a saucepan, fry the onions and garlic until soft and golden. Add the instant potato, stir in all the spices and lemon juice. Pour on the strained coconut milk and slowly bring to the boil, stirring constantly. Simmer for about 15 minutes, add prawns and salt and continue to cook for a further 10 minutes.

Pour into a hot dish, garnish with lemon wedges and serve with saffron rice (see page 20), dishes of sliced banana, and cucumber cooler (see page 71).

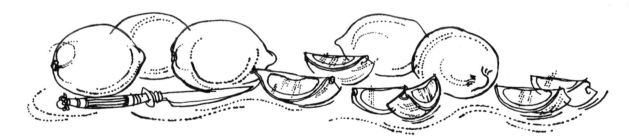

Thai prawn kebab curry

Cooking time: 30 minutes
Serves: 4–6

IMPERIAL	METRIC	AMERICAN
2 lb. prawns	1 kg. prawns	2 lb. prawns or shrimp
8 oz. button onions	225 g. button onions	½ lb. tiny onions
1 large red pepper	1 large red pepper	1 large red pepper
1-inch piece green ginger, sliced (see page 30)	2.5-cm. piece green ginger, sliced (see page 30)	1-inch piece green ginger, sliced (see page 30)
¼ pint oil	1½ dl. oil	⅔ cup oil
1 small onion, grated	1 small onion, grated	1 small onion, grated
2 garlic cloves, crushed	2 garlic cloves, crushed	2 garlic cloves, crushed
2 teaspoons turmeric	2 teaspoons turmeric	2 teaspoons turmeric
¼ teaspoon chilli powder	¼ teaspoon chilli powder	¼ teaspoon chili powder

Shell prawns. Thread on to small skewers alternately with the halved onions, chunks of red pepper, and slices of ginger. Heat oil in large frying pan. Fry grated onion and crushed garlic with turmeric and chilli powder about 15 minutes. Add the kebabs, cook over medium heat, turning skewers from time to time. When prawns are heated through, curry is ready. Serve with rice.

Note. If skewers are unavailable, place kebab ingredients in frying pan as above and cook, stirring occasionally. Serve spooned over rice.

Seafood curry

Cooking time: 45 minutes
Serves: 4–6

IMPERIAL	METRIC	AMERICAN
1 lb. sole fillets, skinned	450 g. sole fillets, skinned	1 lb. sole fillets, skinned
juice of ½ lemon	juice of ½ lemon	juice of ½ lemon
¼ pint water	1½ dl. water	⅔ cup water
1½ oz. butter	40 g. butter	3 tablespoons butter
1 tablespoon curry powder	1 tablespoon curry powder	1 tablespoon curry powder
2 teaspoons grated lemon rind	2 teaspoons grated lemon rind	2 teaspoons grated lemon rind
2 teaspoons flour	2 teaspoons flour	2 teaspoons flour
½ pint light stock	3 dl. light stock	1¼ cups light stock
seasoning	seasoning	seasoning
2 oz. sultanas	50 g. sultanas	⅓ cup seedless white raisins
2 pears	2 pears	2 pears
4 oz. peeled prawns	110 g. peeled prawns	⅔ cup shelled prawns *or* shrimp
3 tomatoes, cut into wedges	3 tomatoes, cut into wedges	3 tomatoes, cut into wedges

Cut the sole fillets into thin strips and tie into 'knots'. Poach gently in lemon juice and water until tender. Drain the fish, reserving the cooking liquid. Melt the butter, add the curry powder and lemon rind, and cook 1–2 minutes. Stir in the flour and cook for further 2 minutes. Gradually add the fish liquid and stock, seasoning and sultanas. Simmer for 15 minutes. Add the sole 'knots', peeled and sliced pears, prawns and tomato, and simmer together for 10 minutes.

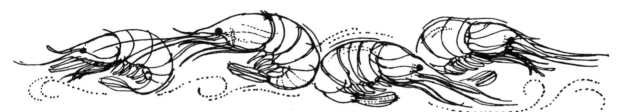

Malay curried shrimps

Cooking time: 1 hour
Serves: 4

IMPERIAL	METRIC	AMERICAN
1 lb. fresh shrimps	450 g. fresh shrimps	1 lb. fresh shrimp
1½ pints water	scant 1 litre water	3¾ cups water
salt	salt	salt
1 onion, grated	1 onion, grated	1 onion, grated
2 tablespoons vegetable oil	2 tablespoons vegetable oil	3 tablespoons vegetable oil
1 teaspoon curry powder	1 teaspoon curry powder	1 teaspoon curry powder
1 garlic clove, crushed	1 garlic clove, crushed	1 garlic clove, crushed
½ pint coconut milk (see page 11)	3 dl. coconut milk (see page 11)	1¼ cups coconut milk (see page 11)
1 cucumber, diced	1 cucumber, diced	1 cucumber, diced
8 oz. fresh coconut, in small chunks	225 g. fresh coconut, in small chunks	½ lb. fresh coconut, in small chunks
lemon slices	lemon slices	lemon slices

Simmer the shrimps in the water with 1 teaspoon salt for about 5 minutes, or until cooked. Remove the shrimps, shell and devein them, and cut into halves. Boil down the liquid until it measures about ¾ pint (½ litre). Brown the onion lightly in the heated oil and remove onion from pan. Fry the curry powder in the same pan until dark brown. Add the garlic and simmer for 3 minutes, or until a thin paste has formed.

Return the onion to the pan and add the coconut milk and shrimp liquid, cucumber and coconut chunks. Salt to taste. Simmer for 30 minutes, or until cucumber is tender and the sauce reduced to about half. Add the shrimps and heat. Serve hot rice separately with garnishes of lemon.

Spiced fried prawns

Cooking time: 10 minutes
Serves: 6

IMPERIAL	METRIC	AMERICAN
3 teaspoons coriander	3 teaspoons coriander	3 teaspoons coriander
pinch ground ginger	pinch ground ginger	pinch ground ginger
2 teaspoons sugar	2 teaspoons sugar	2 teaspoons sugar
2 garlic cloves, crushed	2 garlic cloves, crushed	2 garlic cloves, crushed
2 teaspoons vinegar	2 teaspoons vinegar	2 teaspoons vinegar
$\frac{1}{4}$ teaspoon salt	$\frac{1}{4}$ teaspoon salt	$\frac{1}{4}$ teaspoon salt
$\frac{1}{2}$ teaspoon black pepper	$\frac{1}{2}$ teaspoon black pepper	$\frac{1}{2}$ teaspoon black pepper
1 lb. peeled prawns	450 g. peeled prawns	1 lb. shelled prawns *or* shrimp
oil for deep frying	oil for deep frying	oil for deep frying

Combine all ingredients, except prawns and oil. Coat prawns with this mixture, leave for three hours. Deep-fry in hot oil, drain on absorbent paper. Serve hot.

Indonesian curried prawns or fish

Cooking time: 30 minutes
Serves: 4

IMPERIAL	METRIC	AMERICAN
1 lb. prawns	450 g. prawns	1 lb. prawns or shrimp
1 tablespoon oil	1 tablespoon oil	1 tablespoon oil
1 medium onion, finely chopped	1 medium onion, finely chopped	1 medium onion, finely chopped
2 garlic cloves, crushed	2 garlic cloves, crushed	2 garlic cloves, crushed
1 tablespoon curry powder	1 tablespoon curry powder	1 tablespoon curry powder
$\frac{1}{2}$ pint milk *or* coconut milk	3 dl. milk *or* coconut milk	$1\frac{1}{4}$ cups milk *or* coconut milk
2 oz. thin noodles	50 g. thin noodles	2 oz. thin noodles
1 bay leaf	1 bay leaf	1 bay leaf
1 teaspoon ground coriander	1 teaspoon ground coriander	1 teaspoon ground coriander
1 teaspoon ground caraway	1 teaspoon ground caraway	1 teaspoon ground caraway

Shell and clean prawns. Heat oil, fry onion and garlic 2 minutes. Add prawns, curry powder, coconut milk, noodles, bay leaf, coriander and caraway. Bring to boil, reduce heat, simmer 15 minutes, stirring constantly.

Variation: replace prawns with 1 lb. fish fillets, cut into 2-inch (5-cm.) pieces.

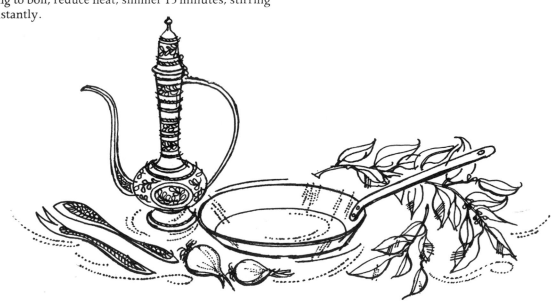

Meat curries

Just as Western meat dishes are prepared in a variety of ways, so are curries. Meats are served as stews, roasts, casseroles, kebabs, etc. The main difference lies in the fact that in curry, spices are used in each dish.

There are too many dishes to list here, but meat curries fall into a few main classes, the names denoting the method of cooking.

Sauce or stew, where meat and/or vegetables are cooked with as little liquid as possible over low heat for a long time. Rice is served separately.

Biriani, a Moslem dish in which meat and rice are cooked together.

Pulao, a dry curry in which raw rice and meat are cooked with whole spices which are left in; all liquid is absorbed in the cooking.

Kebab, portions of meat or meat mixtures are threaded on skewers and barbecued or grilled. They are often basted with hot curried sauces.

Besides these there are many variations of curried dishes such as: *meat balls, hashes, minced cutlets, kormas,* etc.

This section contains typical dishes from each class, and using beef, lamb, pork, veal and offal.

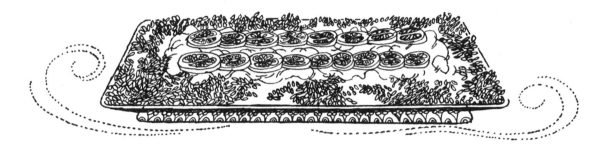

Beef curry favourite

(illustrated on page 27)

Cooking time: 2–3 hours
30 minutes for reheating
Serves: 6

IMPERIAL	METRIC	AMERICAN
¼ pint vegetable oil	1½ dl. vegetable oil	⅔ cup vegetable oil
3 onions, chopped	3 onions, chopped	3 onions, chopped
3 tablespoons curry powder	3 tablespoons curry powder	¼ cup curry powder
2 teaspoons paprika	2 teaspoons paprika	2 teaspoons paprika
1 pint beef stock	½ litre beef stock	2½ cups beef stock
½ pint tomato juice *or* small can tomato purée	3 dl. tomato juice *or* small can tomato purée	1¼ cups tomato juice *or* ¼ cup tomato paste
2 sticks celery, chopped	2 sticks celery, chopped	2 stalks celery, chopped
1 tablespoon dried apricot halves	1 tablespoon dried apricot halves	1 tablespoon dried apricot halves
2 lb. lean stewing beef, cubed	1 kg. lean stewing beef, cubed	2 lb. lean stewing beef, cubed
1 bay leaf	1 bay leaf	1 bay leaf
salt	salt	salt

Heat the oil and lightly fry the onion until transparent. Remove onion and cook the curry powder and paprika in the oil, simmer gently for 3 minutes. Return onion, add stock, tomato juice, celery, apricot halves and cook gently for 15 minutes. Add the meat and bay leaf; salt to taste. Cook on low heat for 2 to 2½ hours. Leave over night in a cool place and reheat the next day when required, taking about 30 minutes on a gentle heat. As this is a curry which is best made the day before, it is a useful dinner party dish. Serve it with pulao rice (see page 18), plain boiled rice, chutney, fruit side dishes, such as pineapple pieces and sliced banana with lemon juice, cucumber and tomatoes, and desiccated coconut, to make a festive spread.

Calcutta meat balls

Cooking time: 50 minutes
Serves: 8

IMPERIAL	METRIC	AMERICAN
meat balls	*meat balls*	*meat balls*
2 lb. minced beef	1 kg. minced beef	2 lb. ground beef
3 oz. breadcrumbs	80 g. breadcrumbs	1½ cups bread crumbs
2 tablespoons grated onion	2 tablespoons grated onion	3 tablespoons grated onion
2 teaspoons salt	2 teaspoons salt	2 teaspoons salt
¼ teaspoon chilli powder	¼ teaspoon chilli powder	¼ teaspoon chili powder
½ teaspoon ground turmeric	½ teaspoon ground turmeric	½ teaspoon ground turmeric
1 garlic clove, crushed	1 garlic clove, crushed	1 garlic clove, crushed
⅛ teaspoon ground black pepper	⅛ teaspoon ground black pepper	⅛ teaspoon ground black pepper
1 egg, lightly beaten	1 egg, lightly beaten	1 egg, lightly beaten
4 tablespoons butter *or* mustard oil	4 tablespoons butter *or* mustard oil	⅓ cup butter *or* mustard oil
4 tablespoons water	4 tablespoons water	⅓ cup water
sauce	*sauce*	*sauce*
8 oz. finely chopped cabbage	225 g. finely chopped cabbage	3 cups finely chopped cabbage
4 onions, finely chopped	4 onions, finely chopped	4 onions, finely chopped
4 peppers, finely chopped	4 peppers, finely chopped	4 peppers, finely chopped
2 tablespoons mashed potato	2 tablespoons mashed potato	3 tablespoons mashed potato
¾ pint boiling water	½ litre boiling water	2 cups boiling water
1 teaspoon salt	1 teaspoon salt	1 teaspoon salt
¼ teaspoon ground black pepper	¼ teaspoon ground black pepper	¼ teaspoon ground black pepper
4 tablespoons yogurt *or* sour cream	4 tablespoons yogurt *or* sour cream	⅓ cup yogurt *or* sour cream

Mix the beef, breadcrumbs, onion, salt, chilli powder, turmeric, garlic, pepper and egg together. Shape into small balls and brown in the hot butter in a heavy pan. Add the water and simmer, covered, for 30 minutes.

Meanwhile make the sauce. Put the cabbage, onions, peppers, and mashed potatoes in the boiling water. Simmer for 15 minutes, or until a smooth sauce is formed. Add seasoning last, with the yogurt or sour cream. Pour this over the curried meat balls.

Madras dry curry

Cooking time: 2 hours
Serves: 6

IMPERIAL	METRIC	AMERICAN
6 tablespoons vegetable oil	6 tablespoons vegetable oil	½ cup vegetable oil
2 large onions, chopped	2 large onions, chopped	2 large onions, chopped
5–6 garlic cloves, sliced	5–6 garlic cloves, sliced	5–6 garlic cloves, sliced
2 tablespoons curry paste *or* powder	2 tablespoons curry paste *or* powder	3 tablespoons curry paste *or* powder
2 tablespoons tamarind purée *or* paste (see page 10)	2 tablespoons tamarind purée *or* paste (see page 10)	3 tablespoons tamarind purée *or* paste (see page 10)
2 lb. chuck steak	1 kg. chuck steak	2 lb. chuck steak
salt	salt	salt

Heat oil, fry onions and garlic until golden. Add curry paste or powder, mix thoroughly, then add tamarind purée or paste, and meat, cut into 1-inch cubes. Cover, simmer 1½ to 2 hours or until meat is tender. Add salt to taste.

Indonesian beef, prawn and noodle curry

Cooking time: 25 minutes
Serves: 6

IMPERIAL	METRIC	AMERICAN
1 lb. beef, slivered	450 g. beef, slivered	1 lb. beef, slivered
8 oz. peeled prawns	225 g. peeled prawns	1½ cups shelled prawns or shrimp
8 oz. cooked chicken, sliced	225 g. cooked chicken, sliced	½ lb. cooked chicken, sliced
1 tablespoon hot curry sauce or 2 tablespoons curry powder	1 tablespoon hot curry sauce or 2 tablespoons curry powder	1 tablespoon hot curry sauce or 3 tablespoons curry powder
4 oz. butter	110 g. butter	½ cup butter
1 tablespoon chopped celery	1 tablespoon chopped celery	1 tablespoon chopped celery
1 large onion, chopped	1 large onion, chopped	1 large onion, chopped
12 oz. carrots, sliced	350 g. carrots, sliced	4 medium carrots, sliced
6 oz. cabbage, shredded	175 g. cabbage, shredded	2 cups shredded cabbage
½ teaspoon black pepper	½ teaspoon black pepper	½ teaspoon black pepper
1 garlic clove, crushed	1 garlic clove, crushed	1 garlic clove, crushed
1 lb. thin egg noodles, cooked	450 g. thin egg noodles, cooked	1 lb. thin egg noodles, cooked
½ pint chicken stock	3 dl. chicken stock	1¼ cups chicken stock
½ teaspoon salt	½ teaspoon salt	½ teaspoon salt

Mix the beef, prawns, and chicken with curry sauce or powder. Heat butter, fry mixture 5 minutes. Cover, cook further 5 minutes, stirring frequently. Add the vegetables, pepper and garlic. Cook for a further 3 minutes. Put in the cooked noodles, chicken stock and salt. Mix, then cook over low heat for about 7 minutes.

Simple beef curry

(illustrated on page 51)

Cooking time: 35 minutes
Serves: 4

IMPERIAL	METRIC	AMERICAN
4 tablespoons vegetable oil	4 tablespoons vegetable oil	⅓ cup vegetable oil
1 onion, finely chopped	1 onion, finely chopped	1 onion, finely chopped
2 teaspoons curry powder	2 teaspoons curry powder	2 teaspoons curry powder
¼ teaspoon ground ginger	¼ teaspoon ground ginger	¼ teaspoon ground ginger
¾ pint beef stock	scant ½ litre beef stock	2 cups beef stock
1 lb. cooked beef, cubed	450 g. cooked beef, cubed	1 lb. cooked beef, cubed
½ cooking apple, unpeeled, diced	½ cooking apple, unpeeled, diced	½ baking apple, unpeeled, diced
1 teaspoon salt	1 teaspoon salt	1 teaspoon salt

Heat the oil and brown the onion in it; remove onion from pan. Fry the curry powder and ginger until dark brown. Return onion to pan and add the stock, cold meat, apple, and salt. Cover and simmer for 15 minutes, or until only half the liquid remains. If liked, add a few nuts and sultanas.

Serve with boiled rice and various sambals.

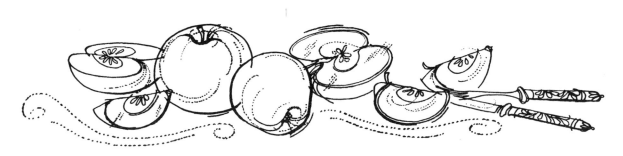

Ceylonese beef badun

Cooking time: 2½–3 hours
Serves: 6

IMPERIAL	METRIC	AMERICAN
2 teaspoons ground coriander	2 teaspoons ground coriander	2 teaspoons ground coriander
1 tablespoon ground cumin	1 tablespoon ground cumin	1 tablespoon ground cumin
2 lb. chuck steak	1 kg. chuck steak	2 lb. chuck steak
1 small onion, sliced	1 small onion, sliced	1 small onion, sliced
2 shallots, sliced	2 shallots, sliced	2 shallots, sliced
5 garlic cloves, chopped	5 garlic cloves, chopped	5 garlic cloves, chopped
1-inch piece green ginger, sliced (see page 30)	2.5-cm. piece green ginger, sliced (see page 30)	1-inch piece green ginger, sliced (see page 30)
2 1-inch pieces cinnamon	2 2.5-cm. pieces cinnamon	2 1-inch pieces cinnamon
¼ pint vinegar	1½ dl. vinegar	⅔ cup vinegar
1 sprig parsley	1 sprig parsley	1 sprig parsley
½ teaspoon chilli powder	½ teaspoon chilli powder	½ teaspoon chili powder
½ pint coconut milk (see page 11)	3 dl. coconut milk (see page 11)	1¼ cups coconut milk (see page 11)
6 oz. coconut cream (see page 10)	175 g. coconut cream (see page 10)	6 oz. coconut cream (see page 10)
2 tablespoons ghee *or* butter	2 tablespoons ghee *or* butter	3 tablespoons ghee *or* butter
salt	salt	salt
lemon juice	lemon juice	lemon juice
green and red peppers	green and red peppers	green and red sweet peppers

Place coriander and cumin in dry saucepan, roast over medium heat until dark chocolate brown in colour. Add meat, cut into 1-inch cubes, and all other ingredients except butter and coconut cream, salt and lemon juice. Bring to boil, cover and simmer 1½ to 2 hours, or until meat is tender. Uncover pan, add coconut cream, simmer further 15 minutes; strain, reserving gravy. Melt butter, fry meat a few minutes, then pour gravy back again and reheat through. Add salt and lemon juice to taste. Serve decorated with slices of green and red peppers.

Beef vindaloo

Cooking time: 2 hours
Serves: 4

IMPERIAL	METRIC	AMERICAN
2 lb. stewing beef	1 kg. stewing beef	2 lb. stewing beef
1 tablespoon ground coriander	1 tablespoon ground coriander	1 tablespoon ground coriander
2 teaspoons ground ginger	2 teaspoons ground ginger	2 teaspoons ground ginger
1 tablespoon ground turmeric	1 tablespoon ground turmeric	1 tablespoon ground turmeric
1 teaspoon ground cumin	1 teaspoon ground cumin	1 teaspoon ground cumin
salt	salt	salt
4 garlic cloves, crushed	4 garlic cloves, crushed	4 garlic cloves, crushed
2 medium onions, chopped	2 medium onions, chopped	2 medium onions, chopped
good ¼ pint vinegar	2 dl. vinegar	good ⅔ cup vinegar
3 tablespoons butter	3 tablespoons butter	¼ cup butter
6 bay leaves	6 bay leaves	6 bay leaves

Cut the beef into 3- to 4-inch pieces. Make a paste of all the spices, garlic, and onions, ground down with vinegar. Rub this over the meat, then leave meat standing in the marinade for 24 hours. Heat the butter and add the meat with marinade and the bay leaves. Simmer over a very low heat until meat is tender and all liquid has gone.

Curry puffs

Cooking time: 1 hour
Serves: 4–6

IMPERIAL	METRIC	AMERICAN
12 oz. minced beef	350 g. minced beef	¾ lb. ground beef
1½ tablespoons oil	1½ tablespoons oil	2 tablespoons oil
2 onions, finely chopped	2 onions, finely chopped	2 onions, finely chopped
1 garlic clove, crushed	1 garlic clove, crushed	1 garlic clove, crushed
2 teaspoons seasoned flour	2 teaspoons seasoned flour	2 teaspoons seasoned flour
2 teaspoons curry powder	2 teaspoons curry powder	2 teaspoons curry powder
juice of ½ lemon	juice of ½ lemon	juice of ½ lemon
1 beef stock cube	1 beef stock cube	1 beef bouillon cube
½ pint hot water	3 dl. water	1¼ cups hot water
2 oz. raisins	50 g. raisins	⅓ cup raisins
2 bay leaves	2 bay leaves	2 bay leaves
12 oz. frozen puff pastry	350 g. frozen puff pastry	¾ lb. frozen puff paste
1 small beaten egg	1 small beaten egg	1 small beaten egg

Brown the meat in hot oil with the onion and garlic. Sprinkle the flour over the meat. Add curry powder and cook for 3 minutes in a corner of pan, then add the lemon juice to mix it into a smooth paste. Make up the stock by crumbling the beef stock cube in the hot water. Pour over the meat, add raisins and bay leaves. Simmer uncovered for 30 minutes, until the meat is tender and the sauce reduced and thick. Remove bay leaves.

Roll out the pastry and cut into rounds with a 6-inch cutter. On each round lay 3 tablespoons of curried beef. Fold the pastry over and carefully seal the edges. Make a slit with a knife for air to escape, and brush each puff with beaten egg. Bake in a pre-heated oven, 450°F., 230°C., Gas Mark 8, for 20 minutes, or until pastry is golden.

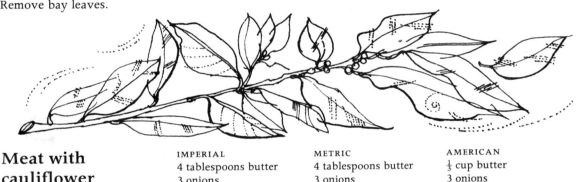

Meat with cauliflower (Gobhi Mhas)

Cooking time: 45 minutes
Serves: 4–6

IMPERIAL	METRIC	AMERICAN
4 tablespoons butter	4 tablespoons butter	⅓ cup butter
3 onions	3 onions	3 onions
2 lb. lean lamb	1 kg. lean lamb	2 lb. lean lamb
1 tablespoon ground turmeric	1 tablespoon ground turmeric	1 tablespoon ground turmeric
1 tablespoon ground coriander	1 tablespoon ground coriander	1 tablespoon ground coriander
1¼ teaspoons ground ginger	1¼ teaspoons ground ginger	1¼ teaspoons ground ginger
2 small tomatoes	2 small tomatoes	2 small tomatoes
4 fl. oz. yogurt	1¼ dl. yogurt	½ cup yogurt
1 lb. cauliflower	450 g. cauliflower	1 small cauliflower
salt	salt	salt
1 teaspoon chilli powder	1 teaspoon chilli powder	1 teaspoon chili powder

Melt the butter in a heavy saucepan. Slice onions and fry them dark brown. Cut the meat into cubes and add with the turmeric, coriander, and ginger. Fry these together for 10 minutes. Add tomatoes and yogurt. Cook until tomatoes are tender. Arrange the cauliflower, cut into small pieces, over the meat.

Mix well, adding salt and chilli powder. Cover and cook. When dry, put in ¼ pint (1½ dl.) water. Cover and continue to cook until the cauliflower is perfectly soft. Simmer 5 minutes over low heat, uncovered. All liquid should be reduced before serving.

Moslem beef kormah

Cooking time: 2¼–4 hours
Serves: 6

IMPERIAL	METRIC	AMERICAN
4 onions, finely chopped	4 onions, finely chopped	4 onions, finely chopped
6 oz. butter	175 g. butter	¾ cup butter
2 lb. beef	1 kg. beef	2 lb. beef
1 teaspoon coriander seeds	1 teaspoon coriander seeds	1 teaspoon coriander seeds
5 cardamom pods, ground	5 cardamom pods, ground	5 cardamom pods, ground
½ teaspoon ground saffron	½ teaspoon ground saffron	½ teaspoon ground saffron
1 teaspoon chilli powder	1 teaspoon chilli powder	1 teaspoon chili powder
4 cloves	4 cloves	4 cloves
1 garlic clove, crushed	1 garlic clove, crushed	1 garlic clove, crushed
1¼ pints water *or* stock	¾ litre water *or* stock	3 cups water *or* stock
1 teaspoon salt	1 teaspoon salt	1 teaspoon salt
½ pint dhal (see page 70)	3 dl. dhal (see page 70)	1¼ cups dhal (see page 70)
1 teaspoon vinegar *or* lemon juice	1 teaspoon vinegar *or* lemon juice	1 teaspoon vinegar *or* lemon juice

Brown the onions lightly in the heated butter and remove from the pan. Cut the meat into small pieces, brown well in the pan, then remove. Mix the spices and fry until dark brown, but do not scorch. Return onions and meat to pan. Add the garlic, water, salt, and dhal. Simmer for 2–4 hours, until meat is very tender. Add the vinegar or lemon juice just before the curry is served. Very little but very rich gravy remains.

Note. The *dhal* can be substituted by the same quantity of canned pease pudding, or condensed pea soup.

Hawaiian curried lamb

Cooking time:
1 hour 15 minutes
Serves: 4–6

IMPERIAL	METRIC	AMERICAN
4 tablespoons butter	4 tablespoons butter	⅓ cup butter
2 teaspoons curry powder	2 teaspoons curry powder	2 teaspoons curry powder
1 tablespoon flour	1 tablespoon flour	1 tablespoon flour
½ pint stock	3 dl. stock	1¼ cups stock
½ pint water	3 dl. water	1¼ cups water
salt	salt	salt
8 oz. cooked lamb, diced	225 g. cooked lamb, diced	½ lb. cooked lamb, diced
8 oz. cooked ham, diced	225 g. cooked ham, diced	½ lb. cooked ham, diced
2 onions, grated	2 onions, grated	2 onions, grated
3 tablespoons raisins	3 tablespoons raisins	¼ cup raisins
1 egg yolk, beaten	1 egg yolk, beaten	1 egg yolk, beaten
¼ pint milk	1½ dl. milk	⅔ cup milk
2 lb. cooked rice	1 kg. cooked rice	6 cups cooked rice

Melt the butter in a heavy pan and brown the curry powder well. Stir in the flour and simmer for a minute until mixture is smooth. Add the stock and water and salt to taste. Put in the top part of a double boiler and add the meats, onions and raisins. Simmer, covered, over boiling water for 1 hour. Stir often.

At the last moment, immediately pan is taken off the heat, stir in the beaten egg yolk and milk. Mix well and pour into the middle of a ring of rice. Serve with bananas and sweet mango chutney.

Curried ham soufflé

Cooking time:
1 hour 45 minutes
Serves: 4

IMPERIAL	METRIC	AMERICAN
4 tablespoons butter or vegetable oil	4 tablespoons butter or vegetable oil	$\frac{1}{3}$ cup butter or vegetable oil
1 small onion, finely chopped	1 small onion, finely chopped	1 small onion, finely chopped
1 teaspoon curry powder	1 teaspoon curry powder	1 teaspoon curry powder
5 tablespoons flour	5 tablespoons flour	6 tablespoons flour
$\frac{1}{2}$ teaspoon dry mustard	$\frac{1}{2}$ teaspoon dry mustard	$\frac{1}{2}$ teaspoon dry mustard
1 pint milk	generous $\frac{1}{2}$ litre milk	$2\frac{1}{2}$ cups milk
1 lb. cooked lean ham, minced	450 g. cooked lean ham, minced	1 lb. cooked lean ham, minced
4 oz. soft breadcrumbs	110 g. soft breadcrumbs	2 cups soft bread crumbs
$\frac{3}{4}$ teaspoon salt	$\frac{3}{4}$ teaspoon salt	$\frac{3}{4}$ teaspoon salt
$\frac{1}{2}$ teaspoon freshly ground black pepper	$\frac{1}{2}$ teaspoon freshly ground black pepper	$\frac{1}{2}$ teaspoon freshly ground black pepper
4 eggs	4 eggs	4 eggs

Heat the butter and brown the onion lightly in it; remove onion from pan. Fry the curry powder until dark brown. Stir in the flour and mustard, simmer for 3 minutes, stirring to a smooth paste. Stir in the milk and simmer until a smooth sauce is obtained. Add the browned onion, minced ham, the breadcrumbs, salt and pepper. Mix well. Separate the eggs. Beat the egg yolks only slightly and blend, a little at a time, with the warm meat mixture. Place over the heat and cook quickly for 1 more minute. Remove from heat and leave to cool while beating the egg whites until they form stiff peaks. Fold whites carefully into the cooled meat mixture and slide the whole gently into a greased baking dish.

Stand it in a shallow pan with 1 inch of water in it. Bake in a moderate oven, 350°F., 180°C., Gas Mark 4, for $1\frac{1}{2}$ hours, or until light and yet slightly firm in the centre.

Kashmir curry

Cooking time:
1 hour 15 minutes
Serves: 6

IMPERIAL	METRIC	AMERICAN
2 lb. boned shoulder of lamb	1 kg. boned shoulder of lamb	2 lb. boned shoulder of lamb
8 fl. oz. sour cream	$2\frac{1}{2}$ dl. sour cream	1 cup sour cream
2 teaspoons garam masala (see page 8)	2 teaspoons garam masala (see page 8)	2 teaspoons garam masala (see page 8)
4 teaspoons curry powder	4 teaspoons curry powder	4 teaspoons curry powder
4 oz. ghee or butter	110 g. ghee or butter	$\frac{1}{2}$ cup ghee or butter
2 tablespoons blanched almonds, slivered or flaked	2 tablespoons blanched almonds, slivered or flaked	3 tablespoons blanched almonds, slivered or flaked
4 oz. sultanas	110 g. sultanas	$\frac{3}{4}$ cup white raisins
4 oz. dried apricots, thinly sliced	110 g. dried apricots, thinly sliced	$\frac{3}{4}$ cup dried apricots, thinly sliced
4 garlic cloves, sliced	4 garlic cloves, sliced	4 garlic cloves, sliced
2-inch piece green ginger, finely chopped (see page 30)	5-cm. piece green ginger, finely chopped (see page 30)	2-inch piece green ginger, finely chopped (see page 30)
2 large onions, sliced	2 large onions, sliced	2 large onions, sliced
salt	salt	salt
lemon juice	lemon juice	lemon juice

Cut meat into 1-inch cubes. Place in bowl with sour cream, garam masala, curry powder; stir well, leave to marinate several hours.

Heat butter in saucepan, fry almonds until golden, remove, drain, and reserve. Fry sultanas and apricots until plumped, remove, and drain. Fry garlic, ginger and onions until golden. Add meat and marinade; cook 5 minutes on medium heat. Add sultanas and apricots; cover and simmer 45 to 60 minutes, until meat is tender; add salt and lemon juice to taste. Garnish with the almonds.

Curried stuffed green peppers with curry sauce

Cooking time:
1 hour 15 minutes
Serves: 8

IMPERIAL	METRIC	AMERICAN
8 green peppers	8 green peppers	8 green sweet peppers
2 tablespoons butter	2 tablespoons butter	3 tablespoons butter
1 large onion, minced	1 large onion, minced	1 large onion, minced
1 garlic clove, crushed	1 garlic clove, crushed	1 garlic clove, crushed
1½ lb. minced lean lamb	700 g. minced lean lamb	1½ lb. ground lean lamb
1 teaspoon curry powder	1 teaspoon curry powder	1 teaspoon curry powder
½ teaspoon ground ginger	½ teaspoon ground ginger	½ teaspoon ground ginger
¼ teaspoon ground cinnamon	¼ teaspoon ground cinnamon	¼ teaspoon ground cinnamon
¼ teaspoon grated nutmeg	¼ teaspoon grated nutmeg	¼ teaspoon grated nutmeg
¼ teaspoon ground coriander	¼ teaspoon ground coriander	¼ teaspoon ground coriander
½ teaspoon salt	½ teaspoon salt	½ teaspoon salt
curry sauce for peppers (see page 50)	curry sauce for peppers (see page 50)	curry sauce for peppers (see page 50)
yogurt	yogurt	yogurt

Wash the peppers and cut off the tops; reserve the tops. Scoop out and discard seeds and membranes. Heat the butter and brown the onion and garlic lightly in it. Add the lamb, curry powder, and all the spices mixed together. Simmer for 5 minutes, then add salt. Fill the peppers with the mixture and fasten on the tops with cocktail sticks. Stand the peppers upright in a baking dish and surround with curry sauce (see page 50). Cover the baking dish and bake in a moderate oven, 350°F., 180°C., Gas Mark 4, for 1 hour, or until meat and peppers are done. If stuffing appears to become dry while cooking, add a little yogurt to the sauce in the bottom of the dish.

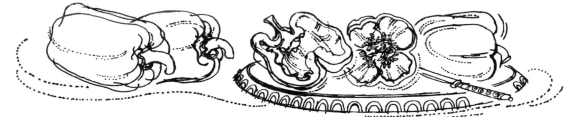

Indonesian grilled lamb on skewers

Cooking time: 30 minutes
Serves: 4–6

IMPERIAL	METRIC	AMERICAN
4 tablespoons peanut oil	4 tablespoons peanut oil	⅓ cup peanut oil
¼ pint vinegar	1½ dl. vinegar	⅔ cup vinegar
¼ pint water	1½ dl. water	⅔ cup water
2 lb. lean lamb, cubed	1 kg. lean lamb, cubed	2 lb. lean lamb, cubed
2 teaspoons ground cardamom	2 teaspoons ground cardamom	2 teaspoons ground cardamom
¼ teaspoon chilli powder	¼ teaspoon chilli powder	¼ teaspoon chili powder
1 teaspoon cumin seeds	1 teaspoon cumin seeds	1 teaspoon cumin seeds
pinch saffron	pinch saffron	pinch saffron
1 teaspoon ground ginger	1 teaspoon ground ginger	1 teaspoon ground ginger
2 garlic cloves, crushed	2 garlic cloves, crushed	2 garlic cloves, crushed
salt	salt	salt
sate sauce (see page 12)	sate sauce (see page 12)	sate sauce (see page 12)

Mix together the peanut oil, vinegar and water. Marinate the lamb in this for one hour. Pound well together the spices, garlic and salt to taste. Drain the meat well. Roll the pieces of meat in the spice mixture. Thread them on skewers, grill on all sides until the lamb is really brown. Serve with sate sauce (see page 12).

Mutton black curry (Ceylon)

Cooking time: 2 hours
Serves: 6

IMPERIAL	METRIC	AMERICAN
1½ lb. stewing mutton	700 g. stewing mutton	1½ lb. stewing mutton
8 oz. lamb's liver	225 g. lamb's liver	½ lb. lamb's liver
1 sheep's heart	1 sheep's heart	1 sheep's heart
butter *or* oil for frying	butter *or* oil for frying	butter *or* oil for frying
1 teaspoon ground cinnamon	1 teaspoon ground cinnamon	1 teaspoon ground cinnamon
1 tablespoon coriander seeds	1 tablespoon coriander seeds	1 tablespoon coriander seeds
2 teaspoons cumin seeds	2 teaspoons cumin seeds	2 teaspoons cumin seeds
1 teaspoon ground cardamom	1 teaspoon ground cardamom	1 teaspoon ground cardamom
15 dry chillis, fried dark and ground	15 dry chillis, fried dark and ground	15 dry chilis, fried dark and ground
saffron	saffron	saffron
1 pint coconut milk (see page 11)	generous ½ litre coconut milk (see page 11)	2½ cups coconut milk (see page 11)
2 garlic cloves, crushed	2 garlic cloves, chopped	2 garlic cloves, chopped
1 large onion, chopped	1 large onion, chopped	1 large onion, chopped
salt	salt	salt
juice of 1 *or* 2 limes, *or* lemon juice	juice of 1 *or* 2 limes, *or* lemon juice	juice of 1 *or* 2 limes, *or* lemon juice

Cut up the meat in small pieces. Fry the spices in a lightly oiled pan until they are very dark. This gives the curry its dark look, hence its name. Put the meat in a saucepan with the coconut milk, spices, garlic, onion and salt to taste. Cook gently until the meat is tender. Add lime juice to taste, stirring it in.

Mild lamb curry

Cooking time: 1½ hours
Serves: 4

IMPERIAL	METRIC	AMERICAN
1 large onion, chopped	1 large onion, chopped	1 large onion, chopped
2 oz. butter	50 g. butter	¼ cup butter
1½ lb. scrag neck *or* shoulder lamb	700 g. scrag neck *or* shoulder lamb	1½ lb. slices *or* shoulder lamb
1 oz. flour	25 g. flour	¼ cup flour
1½ tablespoons curry powder	1½ tablespoons curry powder	2 tablespoons curry powder
1 pint stock	generous ½ litre stock	2½ cups stock
salt and pepper	salt and pepper	salt and pepper
1 tablespoon green chutney	1 tablespoon green chutney	1 tablespoon green chutney
1 banana, sliced	1 banana, sliced	1 banana, sliced
1 oz. raisins	25 g. raisins	3 tablespoons raisins
1 apple	1 apple	1 apple

Sauté chopped onion in the butter until transparent. Cut meat into cubes and toss in flour, add to pan and sauté together with the onion, until lightly browned. Add curry powder, cook further 2 minutes. Gradually stir in the stock, season and simmer for approximately 1¼ hours. Fifteen minutes before the curry is cooked, add chutney, sliced banana, raisins and chopped apple. Serve curry in a shallow bowl, sprinkled with chopped parsley and sultanas, accompanied by boiled rice, apple and banana slices, and mango chutney.

West Pakistani kurma curry

Cooking time:
1 hour 20 minutes
Serves: 4–6

IMPERIAL	METRIC	AMERICAN
1½–2 lb. boned shoulder lamb *or* mutton	¾–1 kg. boned shoulder lamb *or* mutton	1½–2 lb. boned shoulder lamb *or* mutton
1 teaspoon ground coriander	1 teaspoon ground coriander	1 teaspoon ground coriander
1 teaspoon ground cardamom	1 teaspoon ground cardamom	1 teaspoon ground cardamom
1 teaspoon poppy seeds	1 teaspoon poppy seeds	1 teaspoon poppy seeds
1 teaspoon ground cinnamon	1 teaspoon ground cinnamon	1 teaspoon ground cinnamon
1¼ teaspoons ground cloves	1¼ teaspoons ground cloves	1¼ teaspoons ground cloves
1 teaspoon ground black pepper	1 teaspoon ground black pepper	1 teaspoon ground black pepper
½ teaspoon salt	½ teaspoon salt	½ teaspoon salt
2-inch piece green ginger (see page 30)	5-cm. piece green ginger (see page 30)	2-inch piece green ginger (see page 30)
4 garlic cloves	4 garlic cloves	4 garlic cloves
1 onion, finely chopped	1 onion, finely chopped	1 onion, finely chopped
¼ pint yogurt	1½ dl. yogurt	⅔ cup yogurt
2 oz. ghee *or* butter	50 g. ghee *or* butter	¼ cup ghee *or* butter
1 onion, sliced	1 onion, sliced	1 onion, sliced
2 oz. almonds, slivered *or* flaked	50 g. almonds, slivered *or* flaked	½ cup almonds, slivered *or* flaked

Cut lamb into 1-inch cubes. Combine all spices, seasonings, finely chopped ginger, crushed garlic, onion, and yogurt. Place meat in this marinade, leave several hours. Heat ghee, fry sliced onion until golden; remove, then fry almonds, remove and reserve with onion rings for garnish. Drain meat, reserving marinade, add meat to pan and brown well. Add marinade, stir well, cover, and simmer 45 minutes to 1 hour, or until meat is tender. Garnish with the fried onion rings and almonds.

Curried minced lamb

Cooking time: 45 minutes
Serves: 4–6

IMPERIAL	METRIC	AMERICAN
2 lb. leg *or* shoulder lamb	1 kg. leg *or* shoulder lamb	2 lb. leg *or* shoulder lamb
1–2 tablespoons vegetable oil	1–2 tablespoons vegetable oil	2 tablespoons vegetable oil
1 onion, finely chopped	1 onion, finely chopped	1 onion, finely chopped
1 garlic clove, chopped	1 garlic clove, chopped	1 garlic clove, chopped
1 dessert apple	1 dessert apple	1 dessert apple
3 tablespoons curry powder	3 tablespoons curry powder	¼ cup curry powder
2 teaspoons curry paste	2 teaspoons curry paste	2 teaspoons curry paste
1 tablespoon chutney	1 tablespoon chutney	1 tablespoon chutney
2 tablespoons sultanas	2 tablespoons sultanas	3 tablespoons seedless white raisins
salt and pepper	salt and pepper	salt and pepper
2 teaspoons cornflour	2 teaspoons cornflour	2 teaspoons cornstarch
2 tablespoons water	2 tablespoons water	3 tablespoons water

Prepare and mince the lamb. Heat the oil in a pan then fry the mince, finely chopped onion and garlic. Peel and chop the apple and add it to the mince with the curry powder, curry paste, chutney, sultanas and seasoning. Stir well, then cover the pan and simmer gently for about 30 minutes. Blend the corn-flour with the water and gradually pour into the curry, stirring all the time, until the curry is slightly thickened.

Serve in a dish with a border of rice and garnished with slices of cooked tomatoes.

Indonesian fried rice dish (with pork and prawns)

Cooking time: 30 minutes
Serves: 6

IMPERIAL	METRIC	AMERICAN
3 garlic cloves, crushed	3 garlic cloves, crushed	3 garlic cloves, crushed
2 large onions, finely chopped	2 large onions, finely chopped	2 large onions, finely chopped
¼ teaspoon chilli powder	¼ teaspoon chilli powder	¼ teaspoon chili powder
4 tablespoons peanut oil	4 tablespoons peanut oil	⅓ cup peanut oil
1 lb. lean pork	450 g. lean pork	1 lb. lean pork
1 pimiento, finely sliced	1 pimiento, finely sliced	1 pimiento, finely sliced
1 teaspoon turmeric	1 teaspoon turmeric	1 teaspoon turmeric
1 teaspoon ground ginger	1 teaspoon ground ginger	1 teaspoon ground ginger
salt and pepper	salt and pepper	salt and pepper
1½ lb. cooked rice	700 g. cooked rice	4½ cups cooked rice
1 pint peeled prawns *or* shrimps	generous ½ litre peeled prawns *or* shrimps	2½ cups shelled prawns *or* shrimp
8 oz. cooked green peas	225 g. cooked green peas	1½ cups cooked green peas
¼ pint stock	1½ dl. stock	⅔ cup stock

In a large pan, fry the garlic, onions and chilli powder in hot peanut oil. When onions have softened, push them to one side of the pan, add the pork – cut in 1-inch cubes – and fry until brown. Add pimiento, sprinkle in the turmeric, ginger and salt, season highly with pepper. Now add the rice, which should be cold.

Stir it in thoroughly so that the mixture is evenly coloured yellow by the turmeric. Cook and stir for 5 minutes. Add the prawns, peas and stock. Cook for 5 minutes stirring constantly.

Serve with a flat omelette (see page 62) cut in strips and placed on top of the rice.

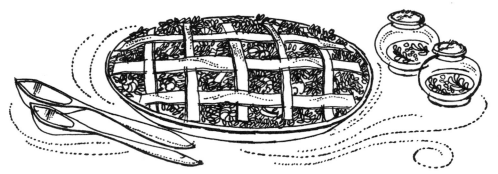

Australian curried rabbit

Cooking time: 2–3 hours
Serves: 6

IMPERIAL	METRIC	AMERICAN
1 rabbit, skinned	1 rabbit, skinned	1 rabbit, skinned
4 tablespoons vegetable oil	4 tablespoons vegetable oil	⅓ cup vegetable oil
2 large onions, finely chopped	2 large onions, finely chopped	2 large onions, finely chopped
1 tablespoon curry powder	1 tablespoon curry powder	1 tablespoon curry powder
1 teaspoon flour	1 teaspoon flour	1 teaspoon flour
1 teaspoon curry paste	1 teaspoon curry paste	1 teaspoon curry paste
¾ pint beef *or* chicken stock	scant ½ litre beef *or* chicken stock	2 cups beef *or* chicken stock
1 cooking apple, grated	1 cooking apple, grated	1 baking apple, grated
1 teaspoon salt	1 teaspoon salt	1 teaspoon salt

Cut the rabbit into pieces, leaving the bones for flavour. Heat the oil in a large saucepan. Brown the onions in the heated oil and remove them from pan, then brown the rabbit pieces quickly and remove them. Fry the curry powder and flour until dark brown. Stir in the curry paste and simmer for a few minutes. Return the onions and rabbit to the pot. Add the stock and apple; season. Simmer until meat is tender, or until the dish is needed.

Ceylonese pork padre curry

Padre curries are for festive occasions. They get their special flavour from a wineglass of whisky. In former times they were made with the local arrack, but nowadays whisky is regarded as being more exclusive. Duck makes a good padre curry.

Cooking time: 1 hour
Serves: 4–6

IMPERIAL	METRIC	AMERICAN
12 pounded dry chillis	12 pounded dry chillis	12 pounded dry chilis
2 teaspoons ground cinnamon	2 teaspoons ground cinnamon	2 teaspoons ground cinnamon
1 teaspoon ground ginger	1 teaspoon ground ginger	1 teaspoon ground ginger
1 tablespoon coconut or peanut oil	1 tablespoon coconut or peanut oil	1 tablespoon coconut or peanut oil
1½–2 lb. lean pork	¾–1 kg. lean pork	1½–2 lb. lean pork
1 bay leaf	1 bay leaf	1 bay leaf
3 tablespoons vinegar	3 tablespoons vinegar	¼ cup vinegar
1 onion, finely sliced	1 onion, finely sliced	1 onion, finely sliced
2 garlic cloves, chopped	2 garlic cloves, chopped	2 garlic cloves, chopped
pepper and salt	pepper and salt	pepper and salt
4 tablespoons whisky	4 tablespoons whisky	⅓ cup whisky
1 tablespoon brown sugar	1 tablespoon brown sugar	1 tablespoon brown sugar
1 pint coconut milk (see page 11)	generous ½ litre coconut milk (see page 11)	2½ cups coconut milk (see page 11)

Fry all the spices in the oil, then mix and pound them together. Cut the pork into small pieces. Put into a heavy pan. Add the spices and other ingredients except whisky and sugar. Cover with coconut milk, simmer very gently for 30 minutes. Add the whisky and sugar, cover and continue to cook slowly until the meat is tender and well cooked.

Remove meat, drain thoroughly, and fry in hot oil until brown. Return to sauce and heat through.

Serve covered with slices of fried potato, and with rice and sambals separately.

Western veal curry

(illustrated on page 63)

Cooking time: 45 minutes
Serves: 4

IMPERIAL	METRIC	AMERICAN
4 tablespoons vegetable oil	4 tablespoons vegetable oil	⅓ cup vegetable oil
1 onion, chopped	1 onion, chopped	1 onion, chopped
1 tablespoon curry powder	1 tablespoon curry powder	1 tablespoon curry powder
2 tablespoons flour or mashed potato	2 tablespoons flour or mashed potato	3 tablespoons flour or mashed potato
½ pint beef stock	3 dl. beef stock	1¼ cups beef stock
½ cooking apple, finely chopped	½ cooking apple, finely chopped	½ baking apple, finely chopped
1 teaspoon salt	1 teaspoon salt	1 teaspoon salt
1 lb. cooked veal, cubed	450 g. cooked veal, cubed	1 lb. cooked veal, cubed
juice of ½ lemon	juice of ½ lemon	juice of ½ lemon

Heat the oil in a heavy pan and lightly fry the onion until transparent; then remove onion. In remaining oil fry the curry powder and flour, allowing it to simmer for 3 minutes. Return the onion; add the stock, apple and salt. Simmer for 20 minutes then add the veal and cook on low heat for another 15 minutes. Add lemon juice just before removing from the heat. Serve on plain boiled rice with tart chutneys.

Goanese pork vindaloo

Cooking time: 2 hours
Serves: 4–6

IMPERIAL	METRIC	AMERICAN
2 large onions, finely chopped	2 large onions, finely chopped	2 large onions, finely chopped
5 garlic cloves, crushed	5 garlic cloves, crushed	5 garlic cloves, crushed
1 teaspoon ground cardamom	1 teaspoon ground cardamom	1 teaspoon ground cardamom
$\frac{1}{2}$ teaspoon chilli powder	$\frac{1}{2}$ teaspoon chilli powder	$\frac{1}{2}$ teaspoon chili powder
1 teaspoon ground cinnamon	1 teaspoon ground cinnamon	1 teaspoon ground cinnamon
2 teaspoons ground cumin	2 teaspoons ground cumin	2 teaspoons ground cumin
2 teaspoons ground turmeric	2 teaspoons ground turmeric	2 teaspoons ground turmeric
2 teaspoons dry mustard	2 teaspoons dry mustard	2 teaspoons dry mustard
3 tablespoons vinegar	3 tablespoons vinegar	$\frac{1}{4}$ cup vinegar
2 lb. lean stewing pork	1 kg. lean stewing pork	2 lb. lean stewing pork
4 tablespoons oil	4 tablespoons oil	$\frac{1}{3}$ cup oil
1 large onion, sliced	1 large onion, sliced	1 large onion, sliced
2-inch piece green ginger (see page 30)	5-cm. piece green ginger (see page 30)	2-inch piece green ginger (see page 30)

Place in a bowl the finely chopped onions, crushed garlic, and all spices. Mix to a paste with a little of the vinegar, divide into 2 portions. To one portion add remainder of vinegar and the pork cut into 1-inch cubes. Leave to marinate 6 hours. Reserve second portion. Heat oil in heavy pan, fry sliced onion, finely chopped ginger, and reserved second portion until onions are golden. Add pork mixture, and bring to the boil, reduce the heat, then simmer $1\frac{1}{4}$ to $1\frac{1}{2}$ hours or until meat is tender, adding a little water only if necessary.

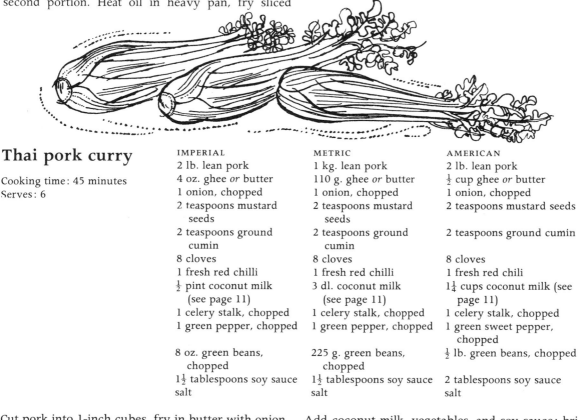

Thai pork curry

Cooking time: 45 minutes
Serves: 6

IMPERIAL	METRIC	AMERICAN
2 lb. lean pork	1 kg. lean pork	2 lb. lean pork
4 oz. ghee *or* butter	110 g. ghee *or* butter	$\frac{1}{2}$ cup ghee *or* butter
1 onion, chopped	1 onion, chopped	1 onion, chopped
2 teaspoons mustard seeds	2 teaspoons mustard seeds	2 teaspoons mustard seeds
2 teaspoons ground cumin	2 teaspoons ground cumin	2 teaspoons ground cumin
8 cloves	8 cloves	8 cloves
1 fresh red chilli	1 fresh red chilli	1 fresh red chili
$\frac{1}{2}$ pint coconut milk (see page 11)	3 dl. coconut milk (see page 11)	$1\frac{1}{4}$ cups coconut milk (see page 11)
1 celery stalk, chopped	1 celery stalk, chopped	1 celery stalk, chopped
1 green pepper, chopped	1 green pepper, chopped	1 green sweet pepper, chopped
8 oz. green beans, chopped	225 g. green beans, chopped	$\frac{1}{2}$ lb. green beans, chopped
$1\frac{1}{2}$ tablespoons soy sauce	$1\frac{1}{2}$ tablespoons soy sauce	2 tablespoons soy sauce
salt	salt	salt

Cut pork into 1-inch cubes, fry in butter with onion, mustard seeds, cumin, cloves and chopped red chilli. Continue to cook gently until pork is almost tender. Add coconut milk, vegetables, and soy sauce; bring to the boil. Simmer gently 10 minutes. Season to taste with salt.

Jamaican curried veal

Cooking time: 45–50 minutes
Serves: 6–8

IMPERIAL	METRIC	AMERICAN
4 oz. butter *or* 4 tablespoons vegetable oil	110 g. butter *or* 4 tablespoons vegetable oil	$\frac{1}{2}$ cup butter *or* $\frac{1}{3}$ cup vegetable oil
2 onions, finely chopped	2 onions, finely chopped	2 onions, finely chopped
2$\frac{1}{2}$ lb. pie veal, diced	1$\frac{1}{4}$ kg. pie veal, diced	2$\frac{1}{2}$ lb. stewing veal, diced
2 tablespoons curry powder	2 tablespoons curry powder	3 tablespoons curry powder
$\frac{3}{4}$ pint stock	scant $\frac{1}{2}$ litre stock	2 cups stock
1 teaspoon salt	1 teaspoon salt	1 teaspoon salt
$\frac{1}{4}$ teaspoon ground black pepper	$\frac{1}{4}$ teaspoon ground black pepper	$\frac{1}{4}$ teaspoon ground black pepper
$\frac{1}{2}$ teaspoon ground ginger	$\frac{1}{2}$ teaspoon ground ginger	$\frac{1}{2}$ teaspoon ground ginger
dash Tabasco sauce	dash Tabasco sauce	dash Tabasco sauce
1 tablespoon tomato sauce	1 tablespoon tomato sauce	1 tablespoon tomato sauce
$\frac{1}{8}$ teaspoon chilli powder	$\frac{1}{8}$ teaspoon chilli powder	$\frac{1}{8}$ teaspoon chili powder
4 tablespoons molasses	4 tablespoons molasses	$\frac{1}{3}$ cup molasses
2 apples, finely chopped	2 apples, finely chopped	2 apples, finely chopped
8 oz. celery, finely chopped	225 g. celery, finely chopped	2 cups finely chopped celery
2 egg yolks, well beaten	2 egg yolks, well beaten	2 egg yolks, well beaten
$\frac{1}{4}$ pint cold water	1$\frac{1}{2}$ dl. cold water	$\frac{2}{3}$ cup cold water

Heat the butter; brown the onions lightly, and remove from the pan. Brown the meat and remove it. Fry the curry powder until dark brown, then return onions and meat to the pan. Add stock, salt, pepper, ginger, Tabasco, tomato sauce, chilli, molasses, apples and celery. Let simmer until meat is very tender, about 30 minutes. Add more liquid if needed to keep meat from sticking, but the mixture should be thick when done. At the last minute mix the egg yolks with the cold water, add to the curry, and cook for another minute or so to thicken.

Serve with lemon wedges, chutney and hot boiled rice.

Vegetable meat curry

(illustrated on the cover)

Cooking time: 1$\frac{1}{4}$ or 2–4 hours
Serves: 4

IMPERIAL	METRIC	AMERICAN
1 onion, grated	1 onion, grated	1 onion, grated
4 tablespoons butter	4 tablespoons butter	$\frac{1}{3}$ cup butter
8 oz. fresh *or* cooked meat	225 g. fresh *or* cooked meat	$\frac{1}{2}$ lb. fresh *or* cooked meat
1 teaspoon curry powder	1 teaspoon curry powder	1 teaspoon curry powder
8 oz. chopped radishes	225 g. chopped radishes	1$\frac{1}{2}$ cups chopped radishes
8 oz. chopped potato	225 g. chopped potato	1$\frac{1}{2}$ cups chopped potato
8 oz. chopped celery	225 g. chopped celery	1$\frac{1}{2}$ cups chopped celery
8 oz. chopped carrot	225 g. chopped carrot	1$\frac{1}{2}$ cups chopped carrot
$\frac{1}{2}$ pint water	3 dl. water	1$\frac{1}{4}$ cups water
1 teaspoon salt	1 teaspoon salt	1 teaspoon salt

Brown the onion lightly in the hot butter and remove onion. Neatly dice the meat, brown it and then remove from pan. Fry the curry powder until dark brown, then add all the other ingredients. If necessary, add more water to cover the mixture. Simmer until vegetables and meat are done – about 1 hour if cooked meat is used, 2 to 4 hours if fresh meat is used. There should be very little gravy in this mixture when served, but it must be rich. Spoon on top of hot boiled rice and serve slices of lemon with it.

Note. Or use any vegetables in season.

Lamb biriani

Cooking time:
2 hours 15 minutes
Serves: 4

IMPERIAL	METRIC	AMERICAN
curry	*curry*	*curry*
1½ lb. lean lamb	700 g. lean lamb	1½ lb. lean lamb
3 thin strips whole ginger	3 thin strips whole ginger	3 thin strips whole ginger
½ teaspoon ground cloves	½ teaspoon ground cloves	½ teaspoon ground cloves
½ teaspoon ground cardamom	½ teaspoon ground cardamom	½ teaspoon ground cardamom
½ teaspoon chilli seasoning	½ teaspoon chilli seasoning	½ teaspoon chili seasoning
1 teaspoon ground cumin	1 teaspoon ground cumin	1 teaspoon ground cumin
¼ teaspoon garlic powder	¼ teaspoon garlic powder	¼ teaspoon garlic powder
1 teaspoon salt	1 teaspoon salt	1 teaspoon salt
½ teaspoon ground black pepper	½ teaspoon ground black pepper	½ teaspoon ground black pepper
½ pint natural yogurt	3 dl. natural yogurt	1¼ cups unflavored yogurt
juice of 1 lemon	juice of 1 lemon	juice of 1 lemon
3 large onions	3 large onions	3 large onions
2 tablespoons oil	2 tablespoons oil	3 tablespoons oil
rice	*rice*	*rice*
8 oz. Patna rice	225 g. Patna rice	1¼ cups long grain rice
¼ teaspoon saffron	¼ teaspoon saffron	¼ teaspoon saffron
8 whole cloves	8 whole cloves	8 whole cloves
8 bay leaves	8 bay leaves	8 bay leaves
12 black peppercorns	12 black peppercorns	12 black peppercorns
½ teaspoon ground cinnamon	½ teaspoon ground cinnamon	½ teaspoon ground cinnamon
½ teaspoon ground cardamom	½ teaspoon ground cardamom	½ teaspoon ground cardamom
6 oz. butter, melted	175 g. butter, melted	¾ cup butter, melted

Trim off excess fat from lamb and cut into 1-inch cubes. Place in the bottom of a large ovenproof casserole. Mix with ginger, ground spices, garlic, salt, pepper, yogurt and lemon juice. Mix thoroughly and leave on one side.

Slice onions and fry in oil until golden brown. Crush half and add to lamb, leaving remaining onions for rice.

Place the rice and spices in boiling salted water and cook for 5 minutes. Drain but do not remove spices. Mix with remaining onions. Spread evenly on top of lamb. Pour over melted butter, cover with tight fitting lid and bake at 350°F., 180°C., Gas Mark 4, for 1 hour. Reduce temperature and bake further 1 hour at 325°F., 170°C., Gas Mark 3. Remove rice to separate plate and keep warm. Arrange lamb on a large oven plate. Cover with rice and garnish with slices of hard-boiled eggs, fried almonds and sultanas.

Curry sauce for peppers

Cooking time: 15 minutes
Makes: about ¼ pint (1½ dl.)

IMPERIAL	METRIC	AMERICAN
2 tablespoons butter *or* vegetable oil	2 tablespoons butter *or* vegetable oil	3 tablespoons butter *or* vegetable oil
1 onion, minced	1 onion, minced	1 onion, minced
1 teaspoon curry powder	1 teaspoon curry powder	1 teaspoon curry powder
¼ pint yogurt	1½ dl. yogurt	⅔ cup yogurt
½ teaspoon salt	½ teaspoon salt	½ teaspoon salt

Heat the butter and fry the onion in it; remove onion. In the same pan, fry the curry powder till dark brown. Return onion and add the yogurt and salt. Simmer for 3 minutes, or until a smooth sauce is formed.

Jhal farzi

Cooking time: 1½–2 hours
Serves: 5–6

IMPERIAL	METRIC	AMERICAN
1½ lb. cooked beef, topside *or* good quality stewing steak	700 g. cooked beef, topside *or* good quality stewing steak	1½ lb. cooked beef, rump *or* good quality stewing steak
2 onions	2 onions	2 onions
1–2 garlic cloves	1–2 garlic cloves	1–2 garlic cloves
1 teaspoon ground ginger	1 teaspoon ground ginger	1 teaspoon ground ginger
1 teaspoon ground coriander	1 teaspoon ground coriander	1 teaspoon ground coriander
½ teaspoon ground turmeric	½ teaspoon ground turmeric	½ teaspoon ground turmeric
¼–1 teaspoon chilli powder	¼–1 teaspoon chilli powder	¼–1 teaspoon chili powder
½–1 teaspoon garam masala	½–1 teaspoon garam masala	½–1 teaspoon garam masala
1 oz. flour	25 g. flour	¼ cup flour
3 oz. butter	75 g. butter	6 tablespoons butter
1 pint stock	generous ½ litre stock	2½ cups stock
grated rind and juice of 1 lemon	grated rind and juice of 1 lemon	grated rind and juice of 1 lemon
1 tablespoon chutney	1 tablespoon chutney	1 tablespoon chutney
1 tablespoon jam	1 tablespoon jam	1 tablespoon jam
2 oz. sultanas	50 g. sultanas	⅓ cup seedless white raisins
coconut milk (see page 11)	coconut milk (see page 11)	coconut milk (see page 11)
seasoning	seasoning	seasoning
2 oz. blanched almonds	50 g. blanched almonds	⅓ cup blanched almonds
Bombay duck (see page 10)	Bombay duck (see page 10)	Bombay duck (see page 10)

Cut the meat into neat pieces. Blend chopped onions and crushed garlic with all the spices and flour, then fry the onion mixture in hot butter for 10 minutes, stirring well. Blend in the stock, lemon rind and juice, sweet chutney, jam and sultanas. Add a little coconut milk, the cooked meat, and season. It should be quite a thick mixture. Cover pan tightly and simmer gently for 1½ hours, stirring from time to time and adding a little extra stock if necessary. Stir in nuts and top with Bombay duck. Serve with poppadums, rice and side dishes.

Simple beef curry (see recipe on page 37)

Poultry curries

Chicken, as well as any fowl such as turkey, duck, pigeon, game birds, etc., is excellent for curries.

Here are recipes from the curry-eating countries, and it will be noticed that each of these has its own special blend of spices for its curries. In South India, for instance, where coconut is used so much, cumin seed and coriander seed are often omitted, as these two spices tend to drown the delicate flavour of coconut.

A large number of recipes deal with chicken, but the same recipes can be used for currying other birds, including game birds like partridges and pheasants.

Assamee chicken curry

Cooking time: 2 hours
Serves: 6

IMPERIAL	METRIC	AMERICAN
3-lb. chicken	1½-kg. chicken	3-lb. chicken
2 oz. butter *or* ghee	50 g. butter *or* ghee	¼ cup butter *or* ghee
salt to taste	salt to taste	salt to taste
1 teaspoon ground black pepper	1 teaspoon ground black pepper	1 teaspoon ground black pepper
2–3 bay leaves	2–3 bay leaves	2–3 bay leaves
1 tablespoon ground turmeric	1 tablespoon ground turmeric	1 tablespoon ground turmeric
pinch chilli powder	pinch chilli powder	pinch chili powder
½ teaspoon ground cloves	½ teaspoon ground cloves	½ teaspoon ground cloves
¾ teaspoon ground cardamom	¾ teaspoon ground cardamom	¾ teaspoon ground cardamom
½ teaspoon ground cumin	½ teaspoon ground cumin	½ teaspoon ground cumin
½ teaspoon ground coriander	½ teaspoon ground coriander	½ teaspoon ground coriander
¾ teaspoon ground ginger	¾ teaspoon ground ginger	¾ teaspoon ground ginger
2 1-inch pieces cinnamon	2 2.5-cm. pieces cinnamon	2 1-inch pieces cinnamon
6–8 garlic cloves, crushed	6–8 garlic cloves, crushed	6–8 garlic cloves, crushed
1-inch piece green ginger	2.5-cm. piece green ginger	1-inch piece green ginger
2 onions, chopped	2 onions, chopped	2 onions, chopped
½ pint chicken stock	3 dl. chicken stock	1¼ cups chicken stock

Joint chicken. Heat butter in saucepan, add all ingredients except chicken, chopped onion, and stock; fry 5 minutes. Add chicken joints, brown well on all sides, then add chopped onion and cook gently, stirring occasionally, 25 to 30 minutes. Gradually add stock, simmer 1 hour, or until chicken is tender. Allow to cool, keep in cool larder or refrigerator overnight. Remove any excess fat, reheat gently.

Chicken in a pot

Cooking time:
2 hours 15 minutes
Serves: 4

IMPERIAL	METRIC	AMERICAN
2-lb. chicken	1-kg. chicken	2-lb. chicken
½ teaspoon chilli powder	½ teaspoon chilli powder	½ teaspoon chili powder
¼ teaspoon ground ginger	¼ teaspoon ground ginger	¼ teaspoon ground ginger
4 oz. long grain rice	110 g. long grain rice	generous ½ cup long grain rice
3 tablespoons chopped green pepper	3 tablespoons chopped green pepper	¼ cup chopped green pepper
2 tomatoes, chopped	2 tomatoes, chopped	2 tomatoes, chopped
4 oz. button mushrooms, halved	110 g. button mushrooms, halved	1 cup button mushrooms, halved
6 tablespoons butter	6 tablespoons butter	½ cup butter
salt	salt	salt
4 mint leaves	4 mint leaves	4 mint leaves
4 onions, sliced	4 onions, sliced	4 onions, sliced
3 teaspoons ground turmeric	3 teaspoons ground turmeric	3 teaspoons ground turmeric
2 tablespoons ground coriander	2 tablespoons ground coriander	3 tablespoons ground coriander
1 teaspoon ground cumin	1 teaspoon ground cumin	1 teaspoon ground cumin

Wash the chicken well and dry it. Prick it all over with a fork and rub in the chilli and powdered ginger. Boil rice in ½ pint (3 dl.) water for 15 minutes. Drain and mix with the green pepper, tomatoes, mushrooms, 1 tablespoon butter, salt to taste and bruised mint leaves. Stuff the chicken with this. Heat remaining butter, brown the onions, then add turmeric, coriander and cumin, and fry the spices for 2 minutes over a very low heat. Put the chicken in and brown it on all sides, mixing well with the spices and onions. Then transfer the chicken to an earthenware casserole, with all the gravy. Sprinkle a little salt and turmeric over and add ¼ pint (1½ dl.) water. Close the lid really tightly and cook in a preheated oven, 300°F., 150°C., Gas Mark 2, for about 1½ hours, until cooked. Add more liquid if necessary. Uncover for the last 5 minutes, raising the heat to high, 425°F., 220°C., Gas Mark 7.

Jade's Malayan chicken curry

Cooking time: 2½–3 hours
30 minutes reheating
Serves: 4

IMPERIAL	METRIC	AMERICAN
6 tablespoons vegetable oil	6 tablespoons vegetable oil	½ cup vegetable oil
4–6 onions, chopped	4–6 onions, chopped	4–6 onions, chopped
4 tablespoons curry powder	4 tablespoons curry powder	⅓ cup curry powder
2 teaspoons paprika	2 teaspoons paprika	2 teaspoons paprika
½ pint water	3 dl. water	1¼ cups water
1 chicken, 3–4 lb.	1 chicken, 1½–2 kg.	1 chicken, 3–4 lb.
1 bay leaf	1 bay leaf	1 bay leaf
salt and pepper	salt and pepper	salt and pepper

Heat oil and fry onions slowly until transparent. Add curry powder and paprika, and cook for 2 minutes. Add water. Over a low heat, and with lid on pan, allow to cook slowly until onions are of a soft, mushy sauce consistency. Add a little more paprika if sauce needs more colour. Joint, wash and dry chicken; put into sauce, add bay leaf, salt and pepper. Leave to simmer very slowly, for 2–3 hours, until chicken is cooked.

Note. The chicken is not fried before going into the sauce, it soaks the spices in better when it is not sealed. Also, this is a curry which improves by being made the day before required; the flavour develops in keeping. Stand in a cool larder overnight, or put into refrigerator when it cools. Reheat slowly for about 30 minutes before needed. Serve with pulao rice (see page 18), pineapple and cucumber sambal (see page 74), and a chutney of your choice.

Indian chicken pulao

Cooking time:
1 hour 20 minutes
Serves: 5–6

IMPERIAL	METRIC	AMERICAN
3-lb. chicken	1½-kg. chicken	3-lb. chicken
1 chicken stock cube	1 chicken stock cube	1 chicken bouillon cube
1 large onion, chopped	1 large onion, chopped	1 large onion, chopped
1-inch green ginger, finely chopped (see page 30)	2.5-cm. green ginger, finely chopped (see page 30)	1-inch green ginger, finely chopped (see page 30)
salt to taste	salt to taste	salt to taste
boiling water	boiling water	boiling water
8 oz. ghee *or* butter	225 g. ghee *or* butter	1 cup ghee *or* butter
3 large onions, finely sliced	3 large onions, finely sliced	3 large onions, finely sliced
2 tablespoons blanched almonds, slivered	2 tablespoons blanched almonds, slivered	3 tablespoons blanched almonds, slivered
4 oz. sultanas	110 g. sultanas	¾ cup seedless white raisins
2 garlic cloves, crushed	2 garlic cloves, crushed	2 garlic cloves, crushed
2 1-inch sticks cinnamon	2 2.5-cm. sticks cinnamon	2 1-inch sticks cinnamon
1 teaspoon ground cardamom	1 teaspoon ground cardamom	1 teaspoon ground cardamom
½ teaspoon ground mace	½ teaspoon ground mace	½ teaspoon ground mace
½ teaspoon ground cloves	½ teaspoon ground cloves	½ teaspoon ground cloves
1 teaspoon ground black pepper	1 teaspoon ground black pepper	1 teaspoon ground black pepper
1 lb. rice	450 g. rice	1 lb. rice
1 teaspoon saffron	1 teaspoon saffron	1 teaspoon saffron

Place chicken in saucepan with chicken cube, chopped onion, ginger, and salt, cover with boiling water, bring to boil, and simmer, covered, 30 minutes. Remove and drain; reserve strained liquid. Melt butter in saucepan, fry sliced onions until golden. Add chicken, brown well on all sides. Add the almonds, sultanas, garlic, and spices except saffron. Then add rice and sufficient chicken stock to cover. Put lid on pan and simmer very slowly, adding more stock, if necessary. Add saffron when rice is nearly cooked.

To serve, place chicken, either whole or carved into joints, on hot dish and cover with rice. A garnish of sliced hard-boiled eggs can be added.

Curried duck

Cooking time: 3–4 hours
Serves: 4–6

IMPERIAL	METRIC	AMERICAN
1 large duck, 5 lb.	1 large duck, 2¼ kg.	1 large duck, 5 lb.
4 tablespoons vegetable oil	4 tablespoons vegetable oil	⅓ cup vegetable oil
1 tablespoon curry powder	1 tablespoon curry powder	1 tablespoon curry powder
6 garlic cloves, crushed	6 garlic cloves, crushed	6 garlic cloves, crushed
½ teaspoon freshly ground black pepper	½ teaspoon freshly ground black pepper	½ teaspoon freshly ground black pepper
¼ pint vinegar	1½ dl. vinegar	⅔ cup vinegar
2 teaspoons salt	2 teaspoons salt	2 teaspoons salt
¼ green pepper	¼ green pepper	¼ green sweet pepper
½ teaspoon sugar	½ teaspoon sugar	½ teaspoon sugar

Cut the duck into pieces and wash and dry. Heat the oil in a heavy saucepan, and fry curry powder to dark brown. Mix with the garlic, black pepper, vinegar, and salt. Add duck pieces and allow to marinate in a cold place for 3 hours, turning the meat often to get it to soak up the flavour. Remove meat. Heat the oil marinade to very hot. Brown the duck, adding more oil if needed. Finely chop the green pepper and add with a little water. Let the mixture barely simmer, covered, over a very low heat for 3 to 4 hours, until meat is cooked and curry is ready. Add a little water if duck sticks. Add the sugar just before the curry is taken from the heat.

Chicken Madras (see recipe on page 56)

Tandoori chicken

Cooking time: 1½ hours
Serves: 4

IMPERIAL	METRIC	AMERICAN
4 chicken quarters	4 chicken quarters	4 chicken quarters
½ pint natural yogurt	3 dl. natural yogurt	1¼ cups unflavored yogurt
½ teaspoon ground ginger	½ teaspoon ground ginger	½ teaspoon ground ginger
1 tablespoon paprika	1 tablespoon paprika	1 tablespoon paprika
½ teaspoon garlic powder	½ teaspoon garlic powder	½ teaspoon garlic powder
4 bay leaves	4 bay leaves	4 bay leaves
6 peppercorns	6 peppercorns	6 peppercorns
1 tablespoon tomato purée	1 tablespoon tomato purée	1 tablespoon tomato paste
grated rind 1 lemon	grated rind 1 lemon	grated rind 1 lemon
1 teaspoon salt	1 teaspoon salt	1 teaspoon salt

Wash and skin the chicken. Prick well with a fork or skewer. Place in a deep bowl or dish. Place yogurt in bowl, add all other ingredients and mix well. Pour over chicken making sure that the quarters are all completely covered with marinade. Cover tightly with foil and leave for 24 hours. At the end of this time remove bay leaves. To cook chicken, place pieces on wire rack in a roasting tin. Alternatively, the chicken may be pierced with long skewers, with the ends resting on the sides of the tin. Coat each joint with any remaining marinade. Bake in a moderate oven, 325°F., 170°C., Gas Mark 3, for 1½ hours. Continue basting until all the marinade has been used. Remove and serve on heated dish, garnished with sprigs of parsley, or cucumber and lemon slices, with accompanying salads.

Chicken Madras

(illustrated on page 55)

Cooking time:
1 hour 50 minutes
Serves: 4

IMPERIAL	METRIC	AMERICAN
2 large onions	2 large onions	2 large onions
1 tablespoon oil	1 tablespoon oil	1 tablespoon oil
3 tablespoons Madras-style curry powder (see page 7)	3 tablespoons Madras-style curry powder (see page 7)	¼ cup Madras-style curry powder (see page 7)
4 chicken portions	4 chicken portions	4 chicken pieces
2 teaspoons tomato purée	2 teaspoons tomato purée	2 teaspoons tomato paste
½ pint water	3 dl. water	1¼ cups water

Chop onions and cook gently in the oil in a large heatproof casserole 3–4 minutes. Add curry powder and continue to fry gently for 5 minutes, stirring continuously. Add chicken portions and continue frying for 10 minutes, then add tomato purée and water, bring to the boil and bake in a low oven, 325°F., 170°C., Gas Mark 3, for 1½ hours.

Serve with boiled rice, tomato and onion salad, mango chutney and poppadums.

Creamed curry vol-au-vents

Cooking time: 20 minutes
Serves: 4

IMPERIAL	METRIC	AMERICAN
1 oz. butter	25 g. butter	2 tablespoons butter
2 teaspoons curry powder	2 teaspoons curry powder	2 teaspoons curry powder
2 teaspoons dry mustard	2 teaspoons dry mustard	2 teaspoons dry mustard
½ oz. flour	15 g. flour	2 tablespoons flour
¼ pint chicken stock or turkey stock	1½ dl. chicken stock or turkey stock	⅔ cup chicken stock or turkey stock
8 oz. cooked chicken or turkey, chopped	225 g. cooked chicken or turkey, chopped	1½ cups chopped cooked chicken or turkey
¼ pint double cream	1½ dl. double cream	⅔ cup whipping cream
8 2½-inch vol-au-vent cases	8 6-cm. vol-au-vent cases	8 2½-inch vol-au-vent cases

Melt butter in pan, add curry powder, mustard, and flour and cook 1 minute. Remove from heat and gradually stir in chicken or turkey stock (this can be made with chicken cube and water). Return to heat and bring to boil, stirring all the time. Add chicken or turkey. Simmer very gently for about 5 minutes. Remove from heat, stir in cream and adjust seasoning. Heat until piping hot, but do not allow to boil. Pour into heated vol-au-vent cases.

Korma-stuffed chicken

Cooking time: 2–4 hours
Serves: 6

IMPERIAL	METRIC	AMERICAN
1 plump roasting chicken (about 4½ lb.)	1 plump roasting chicken (about 2 kg.)	1 plump roasting chicken (about 4½ lb.)
1 tablespoon butter *or* vegetable oil	1 tablespoon butter *or* vegetable oil	1 tablespoon butter *or* vegetable oil
1 onion, grated	1 onion, grated	1 onion, grated
2 tablespoons korma (see page 12)	2 tablespoons korma (see page 12)	3 tablespoons korma (see page 12)
⅔ recipe pulao for stuffing chicken (see page 20)	⅔ recipe pulao for stuffing chicken (see page 20)	⅔ recipe pulao for stuffing chicken (see page 20)
juice of 2 limes *or* lemons	juice of 2 limes *or* lemons	juice of 2 limes *or* lemons
salt	salt	salt
4 oz. melted butter	110 g. melted butter	½ cup melted butter
½ pint water	3 dl. water	1¼ cups water

Prepare the chicken for stuffing and set aside. Heat the butter in a heavy pan; brown the onion. Remove pan from the heat and add the *korma* and *pulao* and half the lime juice. Season with salt to taste. Stuff the chicken loosely with this mixture and sew or skewer openings. Bake in a moderate oven, 350°F., 180°C., Gas Mark 4, for 2–4 hours, or until meat is tender. Baste often with a mixture of remaining lime juice, melted butter, and water. When the bird is ready, place it on a platter and pour the thick rich liquid and any escaped stuffing around it. Serve with chutney and relishes.

Moorghi khari

Cooking time: 1 hour 45 minutes
Serves: 4–6

IMPERIAL	METRIC	AMERICAN
4 medium onions	4 medium onions	4 medium onions
2 oz. ghee *or* butter	50 g. ghee *or* butter	¼ cup ghee *or* butter
2 garlic cloves, crushed	2 garlic cloves, crushed	2 garlic cloves, crushed
2 cloves	2 cloves	2 cloves
4 cardamom pods	4 cardamom pods	4 cardamom pods
2-inch cinnamon stick	5-cm. cinnamon stick	2-inch cinnamon stick
1 teaspoon ground ginger	1 teaspoon ground ginger	1 teaspoon ground ginger
2 teaspoons ground coriander	2 teaspoons ground coriander	2 teaspoons ground coriander
½ teaspoon ground turmeric	½ teaspoon ground turmeric	½ teaspoon ground turmeric
½ teaspoon ground cumin	½ teaspoon ground cumin	½ teaspoon ground cumin
1 teaspoon ground chillis	1 teaspoon ground chillis	1 teaspoon ground chilis
1 medium sized roasting chicken, jointed	1 medium sized roasting chicken, jointed	1 medium sized roasting chicken, jointed
¾ pint chicken stock	scant ½ litre chicken stock	2 cups chicken stock
salt to taste	salt to taste	salt to taste
2 tablespoons dried milk	2 tablespoons dried milk	3 tablespoons dried milk solids
¼ pint water	1½ dl. water	⅔ cup water

Peel the onions and slice finely into rings; keep on one side a few rings to add as garnish. Melt the ghee or butter in a large saucepan and fry the onions, garlic, cloves and cardamom pods together until onions begin to brown. Stir in the remaining spices, fry the chicken joints until they have coloured all over. Add stock, bring to the boil, adjust seasoning to taste, cover the pan and allow to simmer for about 1¼ hours, until the chicken is tender. Remove from heat and stir in the dried milk reconstituted in the water. Lightly flour the onion rings kept aside and fry in hot fat until golden brown. Drain and sprinkle over curry. Serve with boiled rice and tomatoes in vinaigrette dressing (see page 72).

Egg curries

Eggs are an excellent basis for quickly cooked, simple yet substantial dishes. As they can be stored easily they are a good standby, and one of the most effective ways of using them, should you be catering for unexpected guests, is in a curry. Remember, however, that there is a right way to hard-boil an egg, and they can be spoiled by the wrong method of cooking.

Eggs should always be at room temperature before being lowered into cool water. Bring the water slowly to the boil and then just *simmer* for 20 minutes. Put the cooked eggs under cold running water as soon as they are taken from the heat, then they will be easy to shell.

Coconut curried eggs

(illustrated opposite)

Cooking time: 20 minutes
Serves: 5

IMPERIAL	METRIC	AMERICAN
2 tablespoons grated onion	2 tablespoons grated onion	3 tablespoons grated onion
2 tablespoons ghee *or* butter	2 tablespoons ghee *or* butter	3 tablespoons ghee *or* butter
½ teaspoon ground turmeric	½ teaspoon ground turmeric	½ teaspoon ground turmeric
1 fresh red chilli	1 fresh red chilli	1 fresh red chili
8 oz. fresh shredded coconut	225 g. fresh shredded coconut	2 cups fresh shredded coconut
1 tablespoon lemon juice	1 tablespoon lemon juice	1 tablespoon lemon juice
½ pint coconut milk (see page 11)	3 dl. coconut milk (see page 11)	1¼ cups coconut milk (see page 11)
½ teaspoon salt	½ teaspoon salt	½ teaspoon salt
8 oz. tomatoes, sliced	225 g. tomatoes, sliced	½ lb. tomatoes, sliced
5 hard-boiled eggs, sliced *or* **halved**	5 hard-boiled eggs, sliced *or* **halved**	5 hard-cooked eggs, sliced *or* **halved**

Brown the onions lightly in the heated ghee. Stir in the turmeric and fry for a minute longer. Add the chilli, coconut, lemon juice, coconut milk, salt, and tomatoes. Simmer for 5 minutes, or until a paste is formed. Arrange the egg slices in a baking dish. Spoon the coconut mixture on top of them and place in the oven, 350°F., 180°C., Gas Mark 4, for 10 minutes, or until some of the liquid is absorbed. Serve with bread. **Note.** As red chillis are very hot; you may wish to remove before serving.

Curried scrambled eggs

Cooking time: 25 minutes
Serves: 2

IMPERIAL	METRIC	AMERICAN
4 eggs	4 eggs	4 eggs
2 small onions, grated	2 small onions, grated	2 small onions, grated
4 tablespoons butter	4 tablespoons butter	⅓ cup butter
½ teaspoon curry powder	½ teaspoon curry powder	½ teaspoon curry powder
1 large cooking apple, sliced	1 large cooking apple, sliced	1 large baking apple, sliced
small can tomatoes with juice	small can tomatoes with juice	small can tomatoes with juice
pinch chilli powder	pinch chilli powder	pinch chili powder

Beat the eggs lightly and put to one side. Fry the onions lightly in the heated butter; remove onions from pan. In butter remaining, fry the curry powder to dark brown and let simmer for 3 minutes, until a smooth paste is formed. Return the onions to the pan and add the apple, tomato and chilli powder. Cover and let simmer for 15 minutes, or until the mixture is a smooth sauce. Stir in the beaten eggs and cook until set. Serve this piled on rice or noodles.

Coconut curried eggs (see recipe opposite)

Creamed eggs with curried rice

Cooking time: 50 minutes
Serves: 4

IMPERIAL	METRIC	AMERICAN
½ oz. butter	15 g. butter	1 tablespoon butter
1 large onion, finely chopped	1 large onion, finely chopped	1 large onion, finely chopped
1 apple, finely chopped	1 apple, finely chopped	1 apple, finely chopped
4 oz. Patna rice	110 g. Patna rice	generous ½ cup long grain rice
3 teaspoons curry powder	3 teaspoons curry powder	3 teaspoons curry powder
salt	salt	salt
4 tablespoons raisins or sultanas	4 tablespoons raisins or sultanas	⅓ cup dark or white raisins
¾ pint stock or water	scant ½ litre stock or water	2 cups stock or water
¾ pint white sauce	scant ½ litre white sauce	2 cups white sauce
4–6 hard-boiled eggs	4–6 hard-boiled eggs	4–6 hard-cooked eggs

Melt the butter and cook the onion and apple in it until they begin to soften. Add the rice and cook, stirring, until it starts to colour. Blend in the curry powder, add salt to taste, stir in raisins and pour on the hot liquid. Cover and simmer gently for about 45 minutes until liquid has all been absorbed. Make a creamy white sauce by melting 1¾ oz. (45 g.) butter in a saucepan, add 1½ oz. (40 g.) flour, cook, stirring, for 2 minutes. Then slowly add ¾ pint (scant ½ litre) milk, still stirring. Bring to the boil; season well, cook, keeping smooth by stirring, for 2 minutes. Quarter the hard-boiled eggs lengthwise and heat gently in the sauce. Serve garnished with parsley together with the curried rice and mango chutney.

Tropical omelette

Cooking time: 30 minutes
Serves: 4

IMPERIAL	METRIC	AMERICAN
2 oz. butter	50 g. butter	¼ cup butter
2 onions, finely chopped	2 onions, finely chopped	2 onions, finely chopped
2 green peppers, finely chopped	2 green peppers, finely chopped	2 green sweet peppers, finely chopped
2 tomatoes, chopped	2 tomatoes, chopped	2 tomatoes, chopped
2 ripe bananas, chopped	2 ripe bananas, chopped	2 ripe bananas, chopped
1 tablespoon curry paste	1 tablespoon curry paste	1 tablespoon curry paste
pinch salt	pinch salt	pinch salt
6 eggs	6 eggs	6 eggs

Heat the butter and add onions, peppers and tomatoes. When almost cooked through, add bananas and then the curry paste and salt. Stir until the curry paste is dissolved and oily. Separate the eggs, beat the egg yolks, and beat the whites until stiff, separately. Fold the whites into the yolks and pour over the curried fruit and vegetables in the pan. When it begins to set, divide into 4, so that each segment can be turned over to finish cooking.

Curried stuffed eggs

Cooking time: 15 minutes
Serves: 6

IMPERIAL	METRIC	AMERICAN
2 tablespoons butter	2 tablespoons butter	3 tablespoons butter
1 teaspoon curry powder or paste	1 teaspoon curry powder or paste	1 teaspoon curry powder or paste
2 tablespoons flour	2 tablespoons flour	3 tablespoons flour
½ pint milk	3 dl. milk	1¼ cups milk
1 teaspoon salt	1 teaspoon salt	1 teaspoon salt
6 hard-boiled eggs	6 hard-boiled eggs	6 hard-cooked eggs
2 tablespoons vinegar	2 tablespoons vinegar	3 tablespoons vinegar
½ teaspoon dry mustard	½ teaspoon dry mustard	½ teaspoon dry mustard
2 tablespoons mayonnaise	2 tablespoons mayonnaise	3 tablespoons mayonnaise

Heat the butter and in it fry the mixed curry powder and flour till well browned. Add milk and salt. Stir and simmer until mixture becomes a smooth sauce. Shell and halve the eggs. Remove yolks and mash them in a bowl with the vinegar, mustard, and mayonnaise. The mixture should be light but firm enough to make a filling for egg whites. Stuff egg whites and arrange in a serving dish. Spoon curry sauce over them; there should be just enough to mask each egg.

Curried egg pie

Cooking time: 1 hour
Serves: 6

IMPERIAL	METRIC	AMERICAN
filling	*filling*	*filling*
1 oz. butter	25 g. butter	2 tablespoons butter
1 onion, finely chopped	1 onion, finely chopped	1 onion, finely chopped
2 tablespoons flour	2 tablespoons flour	3 tablespoons flour
1 tablespoon curry powder	1 tablespoon curry powder	1 tablespoon curry powder
¼ pint plus 3 tablespoons water	2 dl. water	¾ cup water
juice of 1 lemon	juice of 1 lemon	juice of 1 lemon
1 medium apple, peeled and chopped	1 medium apple, peeled and chopped	1 medium apple, peeled and chopped
1 tablespoon tomato purée *or* 2 tomatoes, peeled and quartered	1 tablespoon tomato purée *or* 2 tomatoes, peeled and quartered	1 tablespoon tomato paste *or* 2 tomatoes, peeled and quartered
seasoning to taste	seasoning to taste	seasoning to taste
6 hard-boiled eggs, halved	6 hard-boiled eggs, halved	6 hard-cooked eggs, halved
pastry	*pastry*	*pastry*
8 oz. plain flour	225 g. plain flour	2 cups all-purpose flour
1 teaspoon salt	1 teaspoon salt	1 teaspoon salt
2 oz. margarine	50 g. margarine	¼ cup margarine
2 oz. lard	50 g. lard	¼ cup lard
3–4 tablespoons cold water to mix	3–4 tablespoons cold water to mix	¼–⅓ cup cold water to mix

Curry sauce for filling: melt the butter, add onion and fry till pale gold. Stir in flour and curry powder and cook till it bubbles. Add water and stir until smooth. Add remaining ingredients, except eggs, cover and simmer 30 minutes. Cool.

To make pie: sift flour and salt. Rub in fats till mixture resembles fine breadcrumbs. Mix to a stiff dough with water. Knead lightly till smooth, turn on to floured board and divide into two. Roll out half pastry, line a 10-inch (26-cm.) pie plate. Place eggs, cut side down, on pastry to within 1 inch (2½ cm.) of edge. Spread cold curry sauce over and between the eggs. Moisten pastry edge with water. Roll out rest of pastry and cover pie, pressing edges well together to seal. Knock with back of knife, then press into flutes. Brush top with beaten egg or milk and decorate with leaves, cut from trimmings. Bake towards top of hot oven, 425°F., 220°C., Gas Mark 7, for 25 to 30 minutes. Serve with bowls of chutney, tomato and onion slices, orange slices and shredded coconut.

Malayan egg curry

Cooking time: 45 minutes
Serves: 4–6

IMPERIAL	METRIC	AMERICAN
¾ pint chicken stock	scant ½ litre chicken stock	2 cups chicken stock
4 medium onions, sliced	4 medium onions, sliced	4 medium onions, sliced
2 green chillis, sliced	2 green chillis, sliced	2 green chilis, sliced
1 garlic clove, sliced	1 garlic clove, sliced	1 garlic clove, sliced
1 teaspoon ground turmeric	1 teaspoon ground turmeric	1 teaspoon ground turmeric
2 teaspoons curry powder	2 teaspoons curry powder	2 teaspoons curry powder
4 oz. desiccated coconut	110 g. desiccated coconut	1⅓ cups shredded coconut
salt	salt	salt
6 hard-boiled eggs	6 hard-boiled eggs	6 hard-cooked eggs

Place all ingredients, except hard-boiled eggs and salt, in a large saucepan. Bring to boil, simmer 30 minutes. Add salt to taste. Shell hard-boiled eggs and halve lengthwise. Add to sauce, cook gently until heated through. Serve with boiled rice and lemon wedges.

Indian egg curry

Cooking time: 30 minutes
Serves: 4–6

IMPERIAL	METRIC	AMERICAN
2 onions	2 onions	2 onions
2 garlic cloves	2 garlic cloves	2 garlic cloves
8 oz. tomatoes	225 g. tomatoes	½ lb. tomatoes
4 oz. ghee *or* butter	110 g. ghee *or* butter	½ cup ghee *or* butter
1 teaspoon ground ginger	1 teaspoon ground ginger	1 teaspoon ground ginger
2 teaspoons ground coriander	2 teaspoons ground coriander	2 teaspoons ground coriander
1 teaspoon ground turmeric	1 teaspoon ground turmeric	1 teaspoon ground turmeric
¼ teaspoon chilli powder	¼ teaspoon chilli powder	¼ teaspoon chili powder
1 teaspoon ground cumin	1 teaspoon ground cumin	1 teaspoon ground cumin
1 teaspoon paprika	1 teaspoon paprika	1 teaspoon paprika
salt to taste	salt to taste	salt to taste
1 teaspoon garam masala (see page 8)	1 teaspoon garam masala (see page 8)	1 teaspoon garam masala (see page 8)
6 hard-boiled eggs	6 hard-boiled eggs	6 hard-cooked eggs

Peel the onions and garlic cloves. Slice one onion thinly, chop remaining onion with the garlic. Peel and chop tomatoes. Heat the ghee or butter, fry the sliced onion until golden. Remove from heat, add the onion and garlic mixture and the spices, except garam masala; add salt to taste. Return and fry 5 minutes. Add tomatoes, simmer until sauce has reached desired consistency. Add garam masala and shelled and halved hard-boiled eggs, simmer further 5 minutes.

Flat omelette

Cooking time: depends on size of pan

IMPERIAL	METRIC	AMERICAN
little oil for frying	little oil for frying	little oil for frying
1 *or* 2 eggs	1 *or* 2 eggs	1 *or* 2 eggs
pepper and salt	pepper and salt	pepper and salt

Heat the oil in a small frying pan. Beat the eggs and add pepper and salt. Cover the bottom of the pan with a thin layer of egg. Cook slowly for 2–3 minutes. Turn out and keep warm. Continue in this way until all the egg is used up. Cut into ¼-inch (½-cm.) strips. Use to garnish rice dishes.

Burmese egg curry

Cooking time: 40 minutes
Serves: 4–6

IMPERIAL	METRIC	AMERICAN
1 lb. onions, finely chopped	450 g. onions, finely chopped	1 lb. onions, finely chopped
3 garlic cloves, crushed	3 garlic cloves, crushed	3 garlic cloves, crushed
½ teaspoon ground ginger	½ teaspoon ground ginger	½ teaspoon ground ginger
4 tablespoons oil	4 tablespoons oil	⅓ cup oil
1 teaspoon salt	1 teaspoon salt	1 teaspoon salt
½ teaspoon ground turmeric	½ teaspoon ground turmeric	½ teaspoon ground turmeric
1 teaspoon paprika	1 teaspoon paprika	1 teaspoon paprika
2 small cans concentrated tomato purée	2 small cans concentrated tomato purée	½ cup tomato paste
½ pint water	3 dl. water	1¼ cups water
1 tablespoon soy sauce	1 tablespoon soy sauce	1 tablespoon soy sauce
6 hard-boiled eggs, halved lengthwise	6 hard-boiled eggs, halved lengthwise	6 hard-cooked eggs, halved lengthwise

Cook onions, garlic and ginger in oil over a low heat until onions are done but not browned. Stir in salt, turmeric and paprika. Gradually add tomato concentrate mixed with water; bring to boiling point and add soy sauce and egg halves. Cook over low heat until sauce and oil appear to separate and egg whites are tinged with colour of sauce. Serve on hot rice.

Western veal curry (see recipe on page 46)

Vegetable curries and dhal

In the East where there are so many people who do not eat meat, it is natural that a great variety of vegetable dishes should have been evolved over the centuries. However, vegetables are seldom cooked or served as a separate dish. They are usually cooked with curry spices and other ingredients, the less tender vegetables, or those requiring long cooking, being either minced first or added at the outset, while the more tender varieties are added later.

Many vegetables and pulses are dried and stored for later use, to provide for days of dreaded droughts and famines. The most used of these are lentils, beans and peas. These appear often in dishes for they provide the protein in a vegetarian diet. White wheat flour is seldom used in curries. For thickening sauces, the most widely used substance is a flour made from dried peas or lentils. Often no thickening is used, but only a little liquid is added in preparation, and the vegetables are simmered down until they have the required texture.

Vegetables are also used in cutlets and fritters, or they may be stuffed with curry mixtures. In fact, vegetables with spices are used as surprisingly tasty main dishes, instead of being just a mere accompaniment to meats. Some fruits are also treated and served as the vegetables.

There are many vegetables available in the Far East. Some are familiar to us, others are strange. The following recipes include only the familiar.

Bengali aubergine curry

Cooking time: 35 minutes
Serves: 3–4

IMPERIAL	METRIC	AMERICAN
2 oz. ghee *or* butter	50 g. ghee *or* butter	¼ cup ghee *or* butter
2 large onions, sliced	2 large onions, sliced	2 large onions, sliced
2 garlic cloves, thinly sliced	2 garlic cloves, thinly sliced	2 garlic cloves, thinly sliced
1-inch piece green ginger, finely chopped (see page 30)	2.5-cm. piece green ginger, finely chopped (see page 30)	1-inch piece green ginger, finely chopped (see page 30)
1 tablespoon ground coriander	1 tablespoon ground coriander	1 tablespoon ground coriander
1 teaspoon ground turmeric	1 teaspoon ground turmeric	1 teaspoon ground turmeric
¼ teaspoon chilli powder	¼ teaspoon chilli powder	¼ teaspoon chili powder
1 teaspoon ground cumin	1 teaspoon ground cumin	1 teaspoon ground cumin
½ teaspoon dry mustard	½ teaspoon dry mustard	½ teaspoon dry mustard
½ teaspoon fenugreek	½ teaspoon fenugreek	½ teaspoon fenugreek
2 large tomatoes	2 large tomatoes	2 large tomatoes
1 large aubergine	1 large aubergine	1 large eggplant
chicken stock	chicken stock	chicken stock
salt	salt	salt

Heat butter in saucepan, sauté the onions, garlic and ginger until onions are just tender. Add the spices, stir well, continue cooking over low heat 5 minutes. Add peeled and chopped tomatoes and diced aubergine. Pour over stock to cover. Simmer 20 minutes or until aubergine is tender. Do not overcook. Add salt to taste.

Curried apple pie

Cooking time: 1 hour
Serves: 4

IMPERIAL	METRIC	AMERICAN
1 oz. butter	25 g. butter	2 tablespoons butter
2 onions, sliced	2 onions, sliced	2 onions, sliced
1 small red pepper	1 small red pepper	1 small red sweet pepper
½ oz. flour	15 g. flour	2 tablespoons flour
1 tablespoon curry powder	1 tablespoon curry powder	1 tablespoon curry powder
juice of ½ lemon	juice of ½ lemon	juice of ½ lemon
1 chicken stock cube, dissolved in ½ pint water	1 chicken stock cube, dissolved in 3 dl. water	1 chicken bouillon cube, dissolved in 1¼ cups water
1 carrot	1 carrot	1 carrot
2 apples	2 apples	2 apples
2 teaspoons tomato purée	2 teaspoons tomato purée	2 teaspoons tomato paste
1 oz. raisins	25 g. raisins	3 tablespoons raisins
1 tablespoon frozen peas	1 tablespoon frozen peas	1 tablespoon frozen peas
1 tablespoon frozen beans	1 tablespoon frozen beans	1 tablespoon frozen beans
seasoning	seasoning	seasoning
pie top	*pie top*	*pie top*
1 lb. cooked potatoes	450 g. cooked potatoes	1 lb. cooked potatoes
2 tablespoons milk	2 tablespoons milk	3 tablespoons milk
½ oz. butter	15 g. butter	1 tablespoon butter
salt, pepper and nutmeg	salt, pepper and nutmeg	salt, pepper and nutmeg

Melt the butter and fry the onions until slightly golden in colour. Add the sliced pepper and cook for further 2 minutes. Stir in the flour and curry powder and cook until the mixture bubbles. Add the lemon juice and stock. Bring to the boil, stirring constantly. Stir in the sliced carrot, the apples, peeled cored and thickly sliced, the tomato purée, raisins, peas and beans. Heat again to boiling and season well. Cover and simmer for 40 minutes. Turn into a heat resistant dish.

Pie top: cream the potatoes with the milk and butter, and season to taste with salt, pepper and nutmeg. Cover the curry with the potato mix, brown under the grill. Garnish with slices of hard-boiled egg, a sprinkling of paprika and a sprig of parsley.

Curried cauliflower

Cooking time: 30 minutes
Serves: 4

IMPERIAL	METRIC	AMERICAN
1 large cauliflower	1 large cauliflower	1 large cauliflower
½ pint yogurt	3 dl. yogurt	1¼ cups yogurt
1 onion, grated	1 onion, grated	1 onion, grated
2 garlic cloves, crushed	2 garlic cloves, crushed	2 garlic cloves, crushed
1 teaspoon ground ginger	1 teaspoon ground ginger	1 teaspoon ground ginger
1 teaspoon sugar	1 teaspoon sugar	1 teaspoon sugar
2 oz. butter	50 g. butter	¼ cup butter
2 onions, chopped coarsely	2 onions, chopped coarsely	2 onions, chopped coarsely
1 teaspoon salt	1 teaspoon salt	1 teaspoon salt
¾ pint hot water	scant ½ litre hot water	2 cups hot water
½ teaspoon ground cinnamon	½ teaspoon ground cinnamon	½ teaspoon ground cinnamon
¼ teaspoon ground nutmeg	¼ teaspoon ground nutmeg	¼ teaspoon ground nutmeg
¼ teaspoon ground coriander	¼ teaspoon ground coriander	¼ teaspoon ground coriander

Separate the cauliflower into flowerets and rinse. Put the yogurt in a large bowl and add the grated onion, garlic, ginger, and sugar. Add the flowerets to this and let them stand for 2 hours, turning pieces several times. Heat the butter in a large saucepan and brown the chopped onions in it: add the cauliflower with its yogurt dressing. Add salt and water and simmer for about 20 minutes, until the vegetable is tender but not mushy. Most of the liquid should be absorbed and only a small amount of the thick sauce remain. Remove from the heat and sprinkle with mixed cinnamon, nutmeg and coriander.

Indian bean foogath

Cooking time: 40 minutes
Serves: 2–3

IMPERIAL	METRIC	AMERICAN
8 oz. green beans *or* French beans	225 g. green beans *or* French beans	½ lb. green beans
water	water	water
salt	salt	salt
4 small onions	4 small onions	4 small onions
2 tablespoons ghee *or* butter	2 tablespoons ghee *or* butter	3 tablespoons ghee *or* butter
½-inch piece green ginger	1-cm. piece green ginger	½-inch piece green ginger
½ teaspoon ground turmeric	½ teaspoon ground turmeric	½ teaspoon ground turmeric
4 garlic cloves	4 garlic cloves	4 garlic cloves
2 green chillis	2 green chillis	2 green chilis
1 tablespoon desiccated coconut	1 tablespoon desiccated coconut	1 tablespoon shredded coconut

Wash and string beans; slice if using green beans. Place in saucepan with ¼ pint (1½ dl.) water, salt to taste, and two of the onions, finely chopped. Boil until soft, simmer until all the water evaporates, remove from heat. Slice remaining onions and brown in another pan in ghee; add ginger, turmeric, garlic, chillis and beans. Stir 3 minutes, then remove from heat. Add coconut, return to heat for 1 or 2 minutes. **Note.** Instead of beans, spinach or cabbage can be used. If so, substitute black pepper for chillis. The use of turmeric is optional.

Curried aubergines and mushrooms

Cooking time: 20–25 minutes
Serves: 4

IMPERIAL	METRIC	AMERICAN
6 tablespoons vegetable oil	6 tablespoons vegetable oil	½ cup vegetable oil
1½ lb. aubergines	700 g. aubergines	1½ lb. eggplants
8 oz. mushrooms	225 g. mushrooms	½ lb. mushrooms
1 tablespoon ground turmeric	1 tablespoon ground turmeric	1 tablespoon ground turmeric
1 teaspoon chilli powder	1 teaspoon chilli powder	1 teaspoon chili powder
salt to taste	salt to taste	salt to taste

Heat the oil. Cut the aubergines in ½-inch slices, and halve the mushrooms if small, quarter them if large, but leave the tiny button variety whole. Add the turmeric and chilli to the oil and cook over a low heat for 15 seconds. Then add the aubergine and fry it on both sides until done. Add the mushrooms a few minutes before aubergine is ready. Mix in well – they take a few minutes only to cook. Add salt to taste before serving. This is a dry curry.

Curried carrots and peas

Cooking time: 35 minutes
Serves: 4

IMPERIAL	METRIC	AMERICAN
1 lb. carrots, washed	450 g. carrots, washed	1 lb. carrots, washed
salt	salt	salt
½ teaspoon ground cumin	½ teaspoon ground cumin	½ teaspoon ground cumin
1 tablespoon chilli powder	1 teaspoon chilli powder	1 teaspoon chili powder
2 tablespoons butter *or* vegetable oil	2 tablespoons butter *or* vegetable oil	3 tablespoons butter *or* vegetable oil
8 oz. shelled fresh green peas	225 g. shelled fresh green peas	½ lb. shelled fresh green peas

Scrape the carrots and cut them in thin rounds. Boil them in water to cover with 1 teaspoon salt until they are tender but still quite firm; drain. Mix the cumin and chilli powder. Heat the butter and fry the spices to a dark brown in it. Simmer for 3 minutes, adding a little water to keep from scorching. Add the carrots, peas, and extra salt if needed. Cover tightly and simmer over low heat until the peas are tender, adding only a drop or two of water if needed to keep them from sticking. The mixture should be thick and quite dry when spooned out on to hot boiled rice.

Australian fruit curry

Cooking time: 25–30 minutes
Serves: 2–3

IMPERIAL	METRIC	AMERICAN
2 tablespoons butter	2 tablespoons butter	3 tablespoons butter
1 large onion, finely sliced	1 large onion, finely sliced	1 large onion, finely sliced
2 large cooking apples, peeled, cored, sliced	2 large cooking apples, peeled, cored, sliced	2 large baking apples, peeled, cored, sliced
4 bananas, sliced	4 bananas, sliced	4 bananas, sliced
3 slices pineapple, diced	3 slices pineapple, diced	3 slices pineapple, diced
1 red pepper, seeded, thinly sliced	1 red pepper, seeded, thinly sliced	1 red sweet pepper, seeded, thinly sliced
1 tablespoon curry powder	1 tablespoon curry powder	1 tablespoon curry powder
1 tablespoon flour	1 tablespoon flour	1 tablespoon flour
$\frac{3}{4}$ pint water	scant $\frac{1}{2}$ litre water	2 cups water
6 stoned dates	6 stoned dates	6 pitted dates
2 tablespoons sultanas	2 tablespoons sultanas	3 tablespoons white raisins
juice of 1 lemon	juice of 1 lemon	juice of 1 lemon
2 teaspoons sugar	2 teaspoons sugar	2 teaspoons sugar
salt and pepper	salt and pepper	salt and pepper

Heat the butter and fry the onion until transparent, then add apple, banana, pineapple and sweet pepper, and cook together for a few minutes. Blend curry powder and flour and add to pan, cook for 2 minutes. Stir in water then dates and sultanas. Simmer 10 minutes. Fruit should be cooked but not broken up. Add lemon juice, sugar, salt and pepper to taste. Serve in ring of boiled rice.

Curried apples and celery

Cooking time: 40 minutes
Serves: 4

IMPERIAL	METRIC	AMERICAN
4 tablespoons butter _or_ vegetable oil	4 tablespoons butter _or_ vegetable oil	$\frac{1}{3}$ cup butter _or_ vegetable oil
3 lb. unpeeled apples, chopped	$1\frac{1}{2}$ kg. unpeeled apples, chopped	3 lb. unpeeled apples, chopped
1 tablespoon curry powder	1 tablespoon curry powder	1 tablespoon curry powder
$\frac{1}{8}$ teaspoon cayenne _or_ dash Tabasco	$\frac{1}{8}$ teaspoon cayenne _or_ dash Tabasco	$\frac{1}{8}$ teaspoon cayenne _or_ dash Tabasco
8 oz. celery, diced	225 g. celery, diced	$1\frac{1}{2}$ cups diced celery
$\frac{1}{2}$ pint tomato juice	3 dl. tomato juice	$1\frac{1}{4}$ cups tomato juice
1 teaspoon salt	1 teaspoon salt	1 teaspoon salt

Heat the butter and brown the apples lightly in it; remove apples from pan. In the same pan, fry the curry powder (and cayenne if used) to a dark brown, about 3 minutes. Return apples to the pan and add all other ingredients. Cover and simmer for 30 minutes, or until celery is tender. This mixture should be almost dry. Spoon on top of hot boiled rice.

Curried cabbage

Cooking time: 25 minutes
Serves: 4–6

IMPERIAL	METRIC	AMERICAN
2 lb. cabbage	1 kg. cabbage	2 lb. cabbage
$2\frac{1}{2}$ tablespoons butter	$2\frac{1}{2}$ tablespoons butter	3 tablespoons butter
2 teaspoons ground cumin	2 teaspoons ground cumin	2 teaspoons ground cumin
4 tablespoons buttermilk	4 tablespoons buttermilk	$\frac{1}{3}$ cup buttermilk
salt to taste	salt to taste	salt to taste
$\frac{1}{4}$ teaspoon cayenne	$\frac{1}{4}$ teaspoon cayenne	$\frac{1}{4}$ teaspoon cayenne
$\frac{1}{2}$ tablespoon lemon juice	$\frac{1}{2}$ tablespoon lemon juice	$\frac{1}{2}$ tablespoon lemon juice
6 mint leaves	6 mint leaves	6 mint leaves
$\frac{1}{4}$ teaspoon powdered saffron	$\frac{1}{4}$ teaspoon powdered saffron	$\frac{1}{4}$ teaspoon powdered saffron

Shred the cabbage and put it in salt water for $\frac{1}{4}$ hour. Drain well. Melt the butter and add the cabbage and cumin, cooking it over a gentle heat for 10 minutes. Add the buttermilk, salt, cayenne, lemon juice and bruised mint leaves. Stir and cook uncovered. When the liquid is almost boiled dry, add the saffron. Mix well; serve piping hot.

Red cabbage in lemon juice

Cooking time: 35 minutes
Serves: 4

IMPERIAL	METRIC	AMERICAN
2 small red cabbages	2 small red cabbages	2 small red cabbages
8 tomatoes, quartered	8 tomatoes, quartered	8 tomatoes, quartered
salt	salt	salt
4 tablespoons yogurt	4 tablespoons yogurt	⅓ cup yogurt
1 tablespoon ground coriander	1 tablespoon ground coriander	1 tablespoon ground coriander
2 teaspoons ground cumin	2 teaspoons ground cumin	2 teaspoons ground cumin
3 tablespoons butter	3 tablespoons butter	¼ cup butter
1 teaspoon black pepper	1 teaspoon black pepper	1 teaspoon black pepper
¼ pint lemon juice	1½ dl. lemon juice	⅔ cup lemon juice

Separate the cabbage leaves without breaking the cabbages. Mix the tomatoes with a good sprinkling of salt, yogurt, and half the coriander and cumin. Stuff the cabbages with the mixture, removing some leaves where necessary. Tie the cabbages at the top. Heat the butter and roll the cabbage in it, over a gentle heat, for 10 minutes, adding the remaining coriander and cumin. Then cover and cook. When they become dry, sprinkle pepper, salt and lemon juice over the cabbages. Cover tightly and braise. Repeat until done. No water is to be used.

Lentil dhal

Cooking time: 45 minutes
Serves: 2–4

IMPERIAL	METRIC	AMERICAN
8 oz. brown lentils	225 g. brown lentils	1 cup brown lentils
1 large onion, chopped	1 large onion, chopped	1 large onion, chopped
2 green peppers, finely chopped	2 green peppers, finely chopped	2 green sweet peppers, finely chopped
1 oz. butter	25 g. butter	2 tablespoons butter
½ teaspoon ground turmeric	½ teaspoon ground turmeric	½ teaspoon ground turmeric
1 teaspoon salt	1 teaspoon salt	1 teaspoon salt
1 teaspoon dry mustard	1 teaspoon dry mustard	1 teaspoon dry mustard
1 teaspoon ground coriander	1 teaspoon ground coriander	1 teaspoon ground coriander

Soak lentils in cold water for 1 hour; drain. Sauté onion and peppers in butter until tender. Add drained lentils, turmeric, and sufficient water to cover well. Bring to boil, simmer until lentils are tender, adding more water if necessary. Add salt, dry mustard, and coriander; mix well. Mixture should resemble thick soup.

Stuffed vegetable marrow

Cooking time:
1 hour 15 minutes
Serves: 4

IMPERIAL	METRIC	AMERICAN
1 medium onion	1 medium onion	1 medium onion
1½ oz. butter	40 g. butter	3 tablespoons butter
8 oz. minced beef	225 g. minced beef	½ lb. ground beef
1 teaspoon ground coriander	1 teaspoon ground coriander	1 teaspoon ground coriander
1 teaspoon chilli powder	1 teaspoon chilli powder	1 teaspoon chili powder
salt to taste	salt to taste	salt to taste
2 tablespoons yogurt	2 tablespoons yogurt	3 tablespoons yogurt
1 teaspoon garam masala (see page 8)	1 teaspoon garam masala (see page 8)	1 teaspoon garam masala (see page 8)
1 vegetable marrow (2–2½ lb.)	1 vegetable marrow (1–1½ kg.)	1 marrow squash (2–2½ lb.)
1 egg	1 egg	1 egg
8 oz. tomatoes, peeled	225 g. tomatoes, peeled	½ lb. tomatoes, peeled

Slice the onion and fry in butter until pale gold in colour. Add the minced meat and fry, turning, for 5 minutes. Add the coriander, chilli, salt and yogurt, and fry over a gentle heat for another 10 minutes, adding water if mixture looks dry. When meat is cooked sprinkle the garam masala over it.

Wash the marrow; peel fine skin off. Cut a piece off top and scoop out seeds. Add the well beaten egg to the mince and stuff the marrow with the mixture.

Replace the piece cut from the top and secure with cocktail sticks. Grease the marrow, wrap it in foil and bake in a moderate oven for 1 hour at 350°F., 180°C., Gas Mark 4. Make a sauce to serve with it, combining any liquid from the marrow with enough water to make 6 tablespoons liquid, and simmering with the skinned chopped tomatoes, until tomatoes are soft. Season to taste.

Onion pakodas

Cooking time: 25 minutes
Serves: 3–4

IMPERIAL	METRIC	AMERICAN
2 large onions	2 large onions	2 large onions
6 oz. plain flour	175 g. plain flour	1½ cups all-purpose flour
6 oz. ground rice	175 g. ground rice	1 cup rice flour
1 oz. semolina	25 g. semolina	2 tablespoons semolina flour
pinch chilli powder	pinch chilli powder	pinch chili powder
1 teaspoon salt	1 teaspoon salt	1 teaspoon salt
1 teaspoon mixed spice	1 teaspoon mixed spice	1 teaspoon mixed spice
1 teaspoon mixed herbs	1 teaspoon mixed herbs	1 teaspoon mixed herbs
½ teaspoon ground turmeric	½ teaspoon ground turmeric	½ teaspoon ground turmeric
water	water	water
oil for deep frying	oil for deep frying	oil for deep frying

Chop or mince the onions. Sieve the flour and add onions, ground rice, semolina, chilli powder, salt, mixed spice, herbs and turmeric. Mix well by adding water gradually, beating hard all the time until a thick batter is formed. Heat the oil in a deep frying pan. Drop the mixture into the hot oil in small balls, using a teaspoon, and fry until golden brown.

Dhal with tomatoes

Cooking time: 1 hour
Serves: 2–4

IMPERIAL	METRIC	AMERICAN
8 oz. red lentils	225 g. red lentils	1 cup red lentils
1 teaspoon salt	1 teaspoon salt	1 teaspoon salt
2 teaspoons curry powder	2 teaspoons curry powder	2 teaspoons curry powder
4 tomatoes, peeled and chopped	4 tomatoes, peeled and chopped	4 tomatoes, peeled and chopped
2 onions, chopped	2 onions, chopped	2 onions, chopped
1¼ pints stock or water	¾ litre stock or water	3 cups stock or water
1 tablespoon oil	1 tablespoon oil	1 tablespoon oil
1 teaspoon dry mustard	1 teaspoon dry mustard	1 teaspoon dry mustard
1 garlic clove, crushed	1 garlic clove, crushed	1 garlic clove, crushed
2 teaspoons paprika	2 teaspoons paprika	2 teaspoons paprika

Soak lentils in water 1 hour; drain. Place lentils, salt, curry powder, tomatoes, and onions in pan, cover with stock or water. Bring to boil, reduce heat, and simmer, covered, 30 minutes or until lentils are tender, adding more stock or water, if necessary. Add oil, dry mustard, garlic and paprika, and simmer further 10 minutes.

Indian potato chahkee

Cooking time: 35 minutes
Serves: 4

IMPERIAL	METRIC	AMERICAN
1 lb. potatoes	450 g. potatoes	1 lb. potatoes
2 tablespoons oil	2 tablespoons oil	3 tablespoons oil
2–3 onions, sliced	2–3 onions, sliced	2–3 onions, sliced
1 tablespoon curry powder	1 tablespoon curry powder	1 tablespoon curry powder
salt to taste	salt to taste	salt to taste
¼ pint hot water	1½ dl. hot water	⅔ cup hot water

Peel and quarter potatoes. Heat oil in saucepan, fry sliced onions until golden, then stir in curry powder and salt. Add potatoes, cook 10 to 15 minutes. Then add the hot water, simmer until potatoes are quite tender.

Nut and green pea curry

Cooking time: 45 minutes
Serves: 4

IMPERIAL	METRIC	AMERICAN
8 small onions, minced	8 small onions, minced	8 small onions, ground
6 tablespoons butter or vegetable oil	6 tablespoons butter or vegetable oil	½ cup butter or vegetable oil
2 teaspoons curry powder	2 teaspoons curry powder	2 teaspoons curry powder
1 teaspoon cornflour	1 teaspoon cornflour	1 teaspoon cornstarch
1 teaspoon ground ginger	1 teaspoon ground ginger	1 teaspoon ground ginger
2 garlic cloves, crushed	2 garlic cloves, crushed	2 garlic cloves, crushed
4 oz. unsalted ground-nuts (peanuts), cashews or almonds	110 g. unsalted ground-nuts (peanuts), cashews or almonds	¾ cup unsalted groundnuts (peanuts), cashews or almonds
¼ pint coconut milk (see page 11)	1½ dl. coconut milk (see page 11)	⅔ cup coconut milk (see page 11)
1 teaspoon salt	1 teaspoon salt	1 teaspoon salt
1 lb. shelled green peas	450 g. shelled green peas	1 lb. shelled green peas
crisp fried onion rings	crisp fried onion rings	crisp fried onion rings

Brown the onions lightly in the heated butter and remove from the pan. Mix the curry powder, cornflour, and ginger and fry in remaining butter until dark brown. Simmer for about 3 minutes, until a smooth paste is formed. Return the onions and add the garlic, nuts, and coconut milk. Add salt. Simmer this mixture for 15 minutes, then add the green peas. Simmer for 20 minutes longer, or until peas are tender but not mushy. Add more salt if required. Spoon out on top of hot boiled rice and garnish with crisp fried onion rings.

Curried potato cakes

Cooking time: 20 minutes
Serves: 3–4

IMPERIAL	METRIC	AMERICAN
8 oz. cold mashed potato	225 g. cold mashed potato	1 cup cold mashed potato
8 oz. cooked green peas	225 g. cooked green peas	1½ cups cooked green peas
1 tablespoon chopped green chillis	1 tablespoon chopped green chillis	1 tablespoon chopped green chillis
good pinch ground ginger	good pinch ground ginger	good pinch ground ginger
good pinch ground coriander	good pinch ground coriander	good pinch ground coriander
salt to taste	salt to taste	salt to taste
1 beaten egg	1 beaten egg	1 beaten egg
4 oz. butter or vegetable oil	110 g. butter or vegetable oil	½ cup butter or vegetable oil

Mix the potato, peas, green chillis, ginger and coriander together. Add salt to taste. Form into small flat cakes. Dip into beaten egg, and fry in hot butter or oil until well browned.

Dhal for serving with curry

Cooking time: 45–55 minutes
Serves: 4–6

IMPERIAL	METRIC	AMERICAN
8 oz. dried split peas	225 g. dried split peas	1 cup dried split peas
1 onion, grated	1 onion, grated	1 onion, grated
2 tablespoons butter or vegetable oil	2 tablespoons butter or vegetable oil	3 tablespoons butter or vegetable oil
1¼ pints water	¾ litre water	3 cups water

Soak the dried peas in cold water overnight. In the morning drain and let stand to dry. Fry the onion in the butter until soft and transparent, then mix in with the peas. Add the water and let it come to a boil. Turn heat very low, cover, and allow the peas to simmer for about 30 minutes, or until they are soft enough to mash. Salt is not added, as the curried food with which the *dhal* is to be served is usually highly seasoned.

Curry accompaniments

Side dishes or sambals are an essential part of a curry meal. In fact much of the popularity of curry derives from the interesting accompaniments served with it. They can be savoury, sharp, pungent, sweet, salty or tart.

The curry connoisseur combines sweet with sour, pungent with mild, mixing a little of each with mouthfuls of the curry and rice.

The term *sambal* is a Malay word for a condiment, especially one made with pickles, coconut and salted fish or roe, but it is used now for other kinds of savouries as well.

Any of the following sambals make delicious curry accompaniments: fried, chopped bacon; plumped raisins; desiccated coconut – plain or mixed with chopped mint; pickled walnuts; cucumber, chopped, mixed with lemon juice, salt and pepper; chopped hard-boiled egg – plain or mixed with chopped green chillis; slices of banana tossed in butter or dipped in lemon juice, served plain or tossed in coconut; preserved or crystallized ginger; cubed pineapple marinated in coconut milk; onion rings browned in butter; a variety of chutneys; salted peanuts; pickled onions; chopped chives; chopped lemon peel; sliced tomatoes or tomatoes chopped and mixed with chopped onions, a little chopped green chilli, lemon juice, salt and pepper.

Some accompaniments which are called chutneys and pickles are actually uncooked relishes, or briefly cooked mixtures which are not preserved. These fresh chutneys must be eaten on the day they are made.

Chilli sambal

Cooking time: 10 minutes

IMPERIAL	METRIC	AMERICAN
15 red chillis	15 red chillis	15 red chilis
oil for frying	oil for frying	oil for frying
1 onion, sliced	1 onion, sliced	1 onion, sliced
2 Bombay duck (see page 10)	2 Bombay duck (see page 10)	2 Bombay duck (see page 10)
lime *or* lemon juice	lime *or* lemon juice	lime *or* lemon juice
sugar	sugar	sugar
salt	salt	salt

Cut up and de-seed the chillis, fry them with the onion and Bombay duck until the onion has softened. Pound as finely as possible, mix smooth with lime or lemon juice. Add sugar and salt to taste. This is exceedingly hot, so take only a little with your curry.

Coconut sambal

IMPERIAL	METRIC	AMERICAN
2 oz. shelled prawns	50 g. shelled prawns	⅓ cup shelled prawns *or* shrimp
2–3 dried chillis	2–3 dried chillis	2–3 dried chilis
1 tablespoon chopped onion	1 tablespoon chopped onion	1 tablespoon chopped onion
6 oz. desiccated coconut	175 g. desiccated coconut	2 cups shredded coconut
salt	salt	salt
juice of 1 lemon	juice of 1 lemon	juice of 1 lemon

Mince or chop the prawns, chillis and onion very finely. Mix with the coconut, season with salt. Moisten well with the lemon juice.

Cucumber cooler

IMPERIAL	METRIC	AMERICAN
¼ cucumber, diced	¼ cucumber, diced	¼ cucumber, diced
5 fl. oz. natural yogurt *or* sour cream	1½ dl. natural yogurt *or* sour cream	⅔ cup unflavored yogurt *or* sour cream

Mix the cucumber with yogurt or soured cream and serve cold. If liked, sprinkle on a little paprika.

Easy to prepare choice of six sambals

Cottage cheese and coconut

IMPERIAL	METRIC	AMERICAN
8-oz. carton cottage cheese	225-g. carton cottage cheese	1 cup cottage cheese
1 tablespoon desiccated coconut	1 tablespoon desiccated coconut	1 tablespoon shredded coconut

Put cheese into a bowl, and lightly fork the coconut into it. Pile the cheese up in the centre of a large platter or use a divided hors d'oeuvre dish.

Apple in lime dressing

IMPERIAL	METRIC	AMERICAN
1 tablespoon oil	1 tablespoon oil	1 tablespoon oil
1 tablespoon lime juice	1 tablespoon lime juice	1 tablespoon lime juice
2 red-skinned apples	2 red-skinned apples	2 red-skinned apples

Beat together oil and lime juice. Core apples and cut into $\frac{1}{2}$-inch (1-cm.) slices. Toss in dressing and arrange the slices overlapping on the dish.

Loganberries

IMPERIAL	METRIC	AMERICAN
6 oz. fresh loganberries or $7\frac{1}{2}$-oz. can logan-berries	175 g. fresh loganberries or 200-g. can logan-berries	$1\frac{1}{4}$ cups fresh loganberries or $7\frac{1}{2}$-oz. can loganberries

Arrange fresh or strained canned loganberries on the dish.

Mushrooms in lemon juice

IMPERIAL	METRIC	AMERICAN
4 oz. button mushrooms	110 g. button mushrooms	1 cup button mushrooms
juice of $\frac{1}{2}$ lemon	juice of $\frac{1}{2}$ lemon	juice of $\frac{1}{2}$ lemon

Wash mushrooms, slice finely and toss in lemon juice. Arrange overlapping on dish.

Tomatoes in vinaigrette dressing

IMPERIAL	METRIC	AMERICAN
2 tablespoons salad oil	2 tablespoons salad oil	3 tablespoons salad oil
2 tablespoons vinegar	2 tablespoons vinegar	3 tablespoons vinegar
good pinch sugar	good pinch sugar	good pinch sugar
pinch salt and pepper	pinch salt and pepper	pinch salt and pepper
$\frac{1}{2}$ teaspoon French mustard	$\frac{1}{2}$ teaspoon French mustard	$\frac{1}{2}$ teaspoon French mustard
3 medium tomatoes	3 medium tomatoes	3 medium tomatoes
1 very small onion	1 very small onion	1 very small onion

Beat together oil, vinegar, sugar, salt, pepper and French mustard. Slice tomatoes finely and toss in the vinaigrette dressing. Arrange in layers in dish and garnish with a few small onion rings.

Prunes in yogurt

IMPERIAL	METRIC	AMERICAN
5 fl. oz. natural yogurt	1½ dl. natural yogurt	⅔ cup unflavored yogurt
7-oz. can prunes, stoned	200-g. can prunes, stoned	7-oz. can prunes, pitted

Spoon the yogurt on to a dish and arrange the stoned prunes on it.

Javanese spiced cucumber

Cooking time: 10 minutes

IMPERIAL	METRIC	AMERICAN
1 large cucumber	1 large cucumber	1 large cucumber
white vinegar	white vinegar	white vinegar
water	water	water
½ teaspoon curry powder	½ teaspoon curry powder	½ teaspoon curry powder
salt to taste	salt to taste	salt to taste

Peel and slice cucumber, put in saucepan, cover with 2 parts vinegar, 1 part water. Add the curry powder and salt, bring to boiling point. Remove from heat, leave to cool in liquid. Drain well.

Fresh apple chutney

IMPERIAL	METRIC	AMERICAN
2 oz. desiccated coconut	50 g. desiccated coconut	⅔ cup shredded coconut
¼ pint hot milk	1½ dl. hot milk	⅔ cup hot milk
1 oz. salt	25 g. salt	1 tablespoon salt
cold water	cold water	cold water
2 large green apples	2 large green apples	2 large green apples
2 tablespoons finely chopped onion	2 tablespoons finely chopped onion	3 tablespoons finely chopped onion
2 tablespoons finely chopped green pepper	2 tablespoons finely chopped green pepper	3 tablespoons finely chopped green sweet pepper
juice of 1 lemon	juice of 1 lemon	juice of 1 lemon

Soak desiccated coconut in hot milk 20 minutes, drain and discard liquid (this can be used in a curry requiring coconut milk, see page 11). Dissolve salt in bowl of cold water. Peel, core, and chop apples; place in the salted water, let stand 10 minutes. Drain apples, mix with onion, pepper and drained coconut. Place in dish, sprinkle with lemon juice, toss, and serve immediately.

Hot coconut sambal sauce

IMPERIAL	METRIC	AMERICAN
8 oz. freshly grated coconut	225 g. freshly grated coconut	2 cups freshly grated coconut
½ pint water	3 dl. water	1¼ cups water
1 tablespoon finely chopped onion	1 tablespoon finely chopped onion	1 tablespoon finely chopped onion
¼ teaspoon ground ginger	¼ teaspoon ground ginger	¼ teaspoon ground ginger
pinch saffron	pinch saffron	pinch saffron
2 tablespoons lime or lemon juice	2 tablespoons lime or lemon juice	3 tablespoons lime or lemon juice

Soak the coconut in the water for 1 hour. Drain off the liquid and reserve it for use in curries. Mix the pressed-out pulp with the onion, ground ginger and saffron, the lime or lemon juice. This makes a fairly hot relish.

73

Cucumber sambal

Cooking time: 20 minutes

IMPERIAL	METRIC	AMERICAN
1 onion, chopped	1 onion, chopped	1 onion, chopped
2 garlic cloves, chopped	2 garlic cloves, chopped	2 garlic cloves, chopped
1 tablespoon coconut *or* peanut oil	1 tablespoon coconut *or* peanut oil	1 tablespoon coconut *or* peanut oil
1 cucumber, chopped	1 cucumber, chopped	1 cucumber, chopped
10 whole dry chillis	10 whole dry chillis	10 whole dry chilis
1 piece Bombay duck, crumbled (see page 10)	1 piece Bombay duck, crumbled (see page 10)	1 piece Bombay duck, crumbled (see page 10)
1 teaspoon ground ginger	1 teaspoon ground ginger	1 teaspoon ground ginger
1 teaspoon ground cinnamon	1 teaspoon ground cinnamon	1 teaspoon ground cinnamon
juice of 1 lime *or* lemon	juice of 1 lime *or* lemon	juice of 1 lime *or* lemon
$\frac{1}{4}$ pint thick coconut milk (see page 11)	$1\frac{1}{2}$ dl. thick coconut milk (see page 11)	$\frac{2}{3}$ cup thick coconut milk (see page 11)

Fry the onion and garlic in hot oil, add the cucumber and the rest of the ingredients. Simmer until the cucumber is soft. Serve this sambal hot or cold.

Malayan onion sambal

IMPERIAL	METRIC	AMERICAN
2 large onions	2 large onions	2 large onions
2 green chillis	2 green chillis	2 green chilis
2 tablespoons vinegar	2 tablespoons vinegar	3 tablespoons vinegar
salt	salt	salt

Slice onions thinly. Discard all seeds from the chillis and slice thinly. Combine all ingredients, adding salt.

Onion and green pepper sambal

IMPERIAL	METRIC	AMERICAN
2 medium onions, finely sliced	2 medium onions, finely sliced	2 medium onions, finely sliced
1 garlic clove, minced	1 garlic clove, minced	1 garlic clove, ground
1 small green pepper, seeded, finely sliced	1 small green pepper, seeded, finely sliced	1 small green sweet pepper, seeded, finely sliced
juice of 1 lime *or* lemon	juice of 1 lime *or* lemon	juice of 1 lime *or* lemon
salt and pepper	salt and pepper	salt and pepper

Mix all the ingredients together, adding salt and pepper to taste.

Fresh mint chutney

IMPERIAL	METRIC	AMERICAN
4 oz. fresh mint leaves	110 g. fresh mint leaves	$\frac{1}{4}$ lb. fresh mint leaves
1 onion	1 onion	1 onion
1 fresh green chilli	1 fresh green chilli	1 fresh green chili
1 teaspoon sugar	1 teaspoon sugar	1 teaspoon sugar
$\frac{1}{4}$ teaspoon salt	$\frac{1}{4}$ teaspoon salt	$\frac{1}{4}$ teaspoon salt
juice of $\frac{1}{4}$ lemon	juice of $\frac{1}{4}$ lemon	juice of $\frac{1}{4}$ lemon

Mince the mint leaves, onion and chilli together. Add sugar, salt, and lemon juice. Mix well and let stand for a few hours before using. Serve this as a sauce or relish on the day it is made.

Onion chatni

Slice finely some large sweet onions into rings, and sprinkle them with finely chopped chilli peppers, both red and green. Sprinkle vinegar lightly on top. Serve the *chatni* fresh.

Indonesian tomato sambal

Cooking time: 30 minutes

IMPERIAL	METRIC	AMERICAN
1 tablespoon oil	1 tablespoon oil	1 tablespoon oil
2 garlic cloves, crushed	2 garlic cloves, crushed	2 garlic cloves, crushed
1 small onion, finely chopped	1 small onion, finely chopped	1 small onion, finely chopped
3 fresh red chillis *or* $\frac{1}{4}$ teaspoon chilli powder	3 fresh red chillis *or* $\frac{1}{4}$ teaspoon chilli powder	3 fresh red chilis *or* $\frac{1}{4}$ teaspoon chili powder
1 lb. firm tomatoes, sliced	450 g. firm tomatoes, sliced	1 lb. firm tomatoes, sliced
2 chopped leeks	2 chopped leeks	2 chopped leeks
salt	salt	salt
1 tablespoon brown sugar	1 tablespoon brown sugar	1 tablespoon brown sugar
1 teaspoon tamarind sauce (see page 10)	1 teaspoon tamarind sauce (see page 10)	1 teaspoon tamarind sauce (see page 10)
$\frac{1}{4}$ pint thick coconut milk (see page 11)	$1\frac{1}{2}$ dl. thick coconut milk (see page 11)	$\frac{2}{3}$ cup thick coconut milk (see page 11)

Heat oil and fry garlic and onion until tender. Add finely chopped chillis, tomatoes and leeks; fry a few minutes, season with salt, sugar and tamarind sauce. Add coconut milk and bring to the boil; reduce heat, simmer 10 minutes.

Quick tomato-banana chutney

Mix equal amounts of chopped tomato and banana. Add a very finely chopped green chilli. Add salt and a little Worcestershire sauce to taste. Use this fresh chutney on the same day it is made.

Pineapple and cucumber sambal

IMPERIAL	METRIC	AMERICAN
2 tablespoons pineapple tidbits	2 tablespoons pineapple tidbits	3 tablespoons pineapple tidbits
1 pickled cucumber	1 pickled cucumber	1 dill pickle
1 oz. green olives, stoned	25 g. green olives, stoned	3 tablespoons green olives, pitted
2 tomatoes	2 tomatoes	2 tomatoes
1 teaspoon desiccated coconut	1 teaspoon desiccated coconut	1 teaspoon shredded coconut

Put the drained pineapple in a bowl and mix with the sliced cucumber, the olives, the tomatoes cut into quarters and halved. Mix well and sprinkle with the coconut.

Yogurt salad

IMPERIAL	METRIC	AMERICAN
2 tomatoes, skinned and chopped	2 tomatoes, skinned and chopped	2 tomatoes, skinned and chopped
½ cucumber, finely sliced	½ cucumber, finely sliced	½ cucumber, finely sliced
5–6 radishes, sliced	5–6 radishes, sliced	5–6 radishes, sliced
2–3 spring onions, finely chopped *or* 2 teaspoons chopped chives	2–3 spring onions, finely chopped *or* 2 teaspoons chopped chives	2–3 scallions, finely chopped *or* 2 teaspoons chopped chives
½ pint natural yogurt	3 dl. natural yogurt	1¼ cups unflavored yogurt
pinch salt	pinch salt	pinch salt
pinch chilli powder	pinch chilli powder	pinch chili powder
paprika	paprika	paprika

Place all these ingredients, except the paprika, in a bowl, mix together. Chill. Sprinkle with paprika.

Pickles, chutneys and sauces

Chutneys and pickles are important side dishes to serve with curry, and following are recipes for some you can make easily, for your store cupboard. Many of these include apples, since this is a fruit that is always plentiful and lends itself so well to preserving. Although there are some good ready-made varieties of mango chutney, we have given a recipe for this here, as mangoes appear more often in shops these days.

There are also a number of more unusual pickles which may be served with curries, and you will find in the specialist shops a wide selection ready-made to choose from.

Peppered apple rings

Cooking time: 20 minutes

IMPERIAL	METRIC	AMERICAN
4 lb. dessert apples	2 kg. dessert apples	4 lb. dessert apples
2 lb. green peppers	1 kg. green peppers	2 lb. green sweet peppers
3 pints cider vinegar	1½ litres cider vinegar	7½ cups cider vinegar
4 oz. brown sugar	110 g. brown sugar	½ cup brown sugar, firmly packed
2 tablespoons juniper berries	2 tablespoons juniper berries	3 tablespoons juniper berries

Peel and core apples and cut into rings; de-seed peppers and cut into rings. Pack into hot sterilized jars in layers. Bring the vinegar, sugar and juniper berries to the boil, and immediately pour over the apple and pepper rings, allowing it to overflow the jars. Seal at once. The flavour improves if the jars are left for six weeks or more before opening – the vinegar syrup then has time to penetrate fully the apple and peppers.

Tamil date pickle

Cooking time: 10 minutes

IMPERIAL	METRIC	AMERICAN
1 lb. stoned dates	450 g. stoned dates	2½ cups pitted dates
vinegar to cover them	vinegar to cover them	vinegar to cover them
1 teaspoon salt	1 teaspoon salt	1 teaspoon salt
1 teaspoon black peppercorns	1 teaspoon black peppercorns	1 teaspoon black peppercorns
10 cloves	10 cloves	10 cloves
1 dried chilli	1 dried chilli	1 dried chili
1 teaspoon cinnamon	1 teaspoon cinnamon	1 teaspoon cinnamon

Put the dates in jars. If you are using block dates separate them. Boil the vinegar with the salt and spices for 2 minutes. Cool slightly. Pour the spiced vinegar over the dates. Leave until cold then cork the jars securely. Leave for at least two weeks before using.

Minced lemon pickle

Cooking time: 2 hours

IMPERIAL	METRIC	AMERICAN
8 lemons	8 lemons	8 lemons
2 tablespoons salt	2 tablespoons salt	3 tablespoons salt
1 garlic clove, crushed	1 garlic clove, crushed	1 garlic clove, crushed
1 lb. raisins	450 g. raisins	3 cups raisins
1 teaspoon chilli powder	1 teaspoon chilli powder	1 teaspoon chili powder
2 teaspoons ground ginger	2 teaspoons ground ginger	2 teaspoons ground ginger
1¼ pints cider vinegar	¾ litre cider vinegar	3 cups cider vinegar
1½ lb. brown sugar	700 g. brown sugar	3 cups brown sugar, firmly packed

Cut unpeeled lemons into quarters, remove pips, and put lemons in a bowl. Sprinkle the salt over them. Let them stand for 4 days, turning often. Mix the garlic, raisins, chilli powder, and ginger with a little of the vinegar and let stand for 24 hours. Mince or grind the two mixtures together. Add the sugar and the rest of the vinegar and put all into a heavy saucepan.

Simmer until mixture becomes very thick. Leave until cold before bottling. Can be used after 5 days.

Sharp apple chutney

Cooking time: 1 hour

IMPERIAL	METRIC	AMERICAN
4 lb. apples	2 kg. apples	4 lb. apples
1½ lb. onions	700 g. onions	1½ lb. onions
4 oz. raisins	110 g. raisins	¾ cup raisins
4 oz. sultanas	110 g. sultanas	¾ cup seedless white raisins
4 oz. currants	110 g. currants	¾ cup currants
1 lb. brown sugar	450 g. brown sugar	2 cups brown sugar, firmly packed
1 tablespoon black treacle	1 tablespoon black treacle	1 tablespoon molasses
1 pint vinegar	generous ½ litre vinegar	2½ cups vinegar
1 tablespoon salt	1 tablespoon salt	1 tablespoon salt
pinch cayenne	pinch cayenne	pinch cayenne

Peel, core and chop the apples finely; slice the onions, stone and chop raisins and sultanas, clean the currants. Put all in pan with sugar and treacle, vinegar, salt and pinch of cayenne. Simmer gently for 1 hour, stirring frequently. Put into jars with a few spices in each jar (i.e. a few cloves, piece of cinnamon stick, black peppercorns, etc.), and tie down securely.

Apple and nut chutney

Cooking time: 1 hour

IMPERIAL	METRIC	AMERICAN
4 lb. apples	2 kg. apples	4 lb. apples
grated rind of 2 lemons	grated rind of 2 lemons	grated rind of 2 lemons
grated rind of 2 oranges	grated rind of 2 oranges	grated rind of 2 oranges
1 lb. onions, chopped	450 g. onions, chopped	1 lb. onions, chopped
8 oz. walnuts, roughly chopped	225 g. walnuts, roughly chopped	2 cups roughly chopped walnuts
8 oz. hazelnuts, roughly chopped	225 g. hazelnuts, roughly chopped	2 cups roughly chopped hazelnuts
1 pint vinegar	generous ½ litre vinegar	2½ cups vinegar
1 lb. brown sugar	450 g. brown sugar	2 cups brown sugar, firmly packed
3 tablespoons golden syrup	3 tablespoons golden syrup	¼ cup corn syrup
1 tablespoon salt	1 tablespoon salt	1 tablespoon salt
pinch cayenne	pinch cayenne	pinch cayenne

Peel, core and chop the apples. Place all ingredients in a preserving pan. Simmer gently for 1 hour, stirring frequently. Pour the chutney into sterilized jars and seal.

Pear, orange and raisin chutney

Cooking time: 1 hour

IMPERIAL	METRIC	AMERICAN
4 lb. pears	2 kg. pears	4 lb. pears
5 thin-skinned oranges	5 thin-skinned oranges	5 thin-skinned oranges
12 oz. onions	350 g. onions	¾ lb. onions
1 lb. raisins	450 g. raisins	3 cups raisins
1 pint vinegar	generous ½ litre vinegar	2½ cups vinegar
1½ lb. brown sugar	700 g. brown sugar	3 cups brown sugar, firmly packed
2 teaspoons salt	2 teaspoons salt	2 teaspoons salt

Peel, core and chop pears; chop oranges and onions. Place all ingredients in a preserving pan and simmer gently for about an hour, stirring frequently. Put into jars and seal.

Green mango chutney

Cooking time: 1 hour 15 minutes

IMPERIAL	METRIC	AMERICAN
1 lb. green mangoes	450 g. green mangoes	1 lb. green mangoes
salt	salt	salt
1 oz. dry chillis	25 g. dry chillis	¼ cup dry chilis
1 oz. garlic	25 g. garlic	2 tablespoons garlic cloves
½ pint vinegar	3 dl. vinegar	1¼ cups vinegar
1 lb. brown sugar	450 g. brown sugar	2 cups brown sugar, firmly packed
1 oz. bruised root ginger	25 g. bruised root ginger	1 oz. bruised ginger root
1 oz. mustard seeds	25 g. mustard seeds	¼ cup mustard seeds
4 oz. sultanas	110 g. sultanas	¾ cup seedless white raisins

Peel and slice the mangoes, discard the stones. Sprinkle them with salt and leave in a warm, dry place for 24 hours. Pound the chillis and garlic with a little vinegar. Boil the sugar, vinegar, chillis, garlic, ginger, mustard seeds and sultanas until the syrup thickens. Add the mangoes and cook them until they are tender. This takes about 30–45 minutes. Put into warm jars, tie down when cold.

Bengal chutney

Cooking time: 1 hour

IMPERIAL	METRIC	AMERICAN
1 lb. sultanas	450 g. sultanas	3 cups seedless white raisins
1 lb. stoned dates	450 g. stoned dates	2½ cups pitted dates
8 oz. dried apricots	225 g. dried apricots	1½ cups dried apricots
8 oz. dried peaches	225 g. dried peaches	1½ cups dried peaches
1 lb. green tomatoes	450 g. green tomatoes	1 lb. green tomatoes
3 large green apples	3 large green apples	3 large green apples
2 large red chillis *or* red peppers	2 large red chillis *or* red peppers	2 large red chilis *or* red peppers
4 oz. green ginger (see page 30)	110 g. green ginger (see page 30)	¼ lb. green ginger (see page 30)
2 oz. salt	50 g. salt	scant ¼ cup salt
1 lb. brown sugar	450 g. brown sugar	2 cups brown sugar, firmly packed
1 quart vinegar	generous 1 litre vinegar	5 cups vinegar
2 teaspoons allspice	2 teaspoons allspice	2 teaspoons allspice
2 teaspoons whole cloves	2 teaspoons whole cloves	2 teaspoons whole cloves

Put sultanas, dates, apricots and peaches through mincer, or chop finely. Place in pan with chopped, peeled tomatoes, peeled, cored and chopped apples, chopped seeded chillis or peppers, chopped ginger, salt, brown sugar, vinegar, allspice, and cloves. Cook steadily until it reaches thick chutney consistency. Bottle while hot, seal when cold.

Index